Heard the One About Identity Theft?

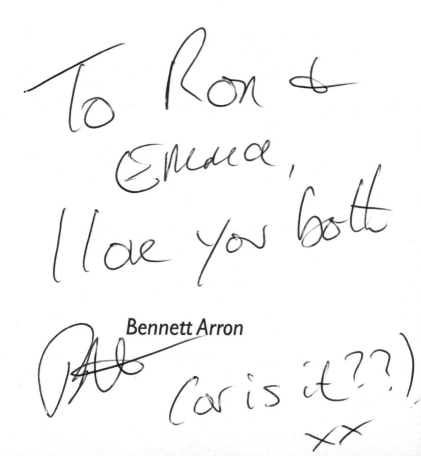

To Ron &
Emma,
I loe you both

Bennett Arron

(or is it??)
xx

Heard The One About Identity Theft?

Published by Silly Papi Ltd 2015

Although this book is a work of non-fiction, one or two of the
names have been changed. Which is ironic for a book about
identity theft.

A catalogue record for this book is available
from the British Library

ISBN: 978-0-9933571-0-7

Printed by CPI Group UK, Croydon CR0 4YY

The Author

His mother's maiden name is Thomas. His PIN is 4321. His date of birth is 01/04/73.

Bennett Arron is a stand-up comedian, BAFTA-shortlisted director and award-winning writer.

He made the critically acclaimed Channel 4 documentary *How To Steal an Identity.*

He has written for several television programmes including *Genie in the House,* which was the highest-rated sitcom on Nickelodeon, and the BBC's BAFTA-winning *The Slammer.* He also presented the documentary *The Kosher Comedian* for the BBC.

He is a familiar face on the UK comedy circuit and has performed around the world at clubs and as an after-dinner speaker

Bennett is a past winner of the BBC New Writers' Award and the TAPS Comedy Writer of the Year Award. In addition to this, he came third in an international disco-dancing championship in Tenerife.

Genuinely original and funny
THE TIMES
Hilarious . . . clever wit . . . razor sharp
STANDARD
One of the best on the circuit . . . a Welsh Seinfeld
THE GUARDIAN

To Rosy. For everything.

Prologue

When I was younger, I kept a daily diary. I would write in it every night describing all the events that had happened that day, regardless of whether or not they were interesting. After all, it wasn't for anyone else to read so I didn't have to worry about it being critiqued. I kept up this diary for many years, and then stopped.

In 2002, it looked as if I was about to have a sitcom script produced on television. I wanted to chronicle the build-up to this and keep an account of what happened. So I started to write a diary again. In doing this, I unexpectedly kept a daily record of a devastating experience that continues to affect my life to this day. Most of the diary excerpts were written on the evening of the day the events took place and so the reactions and emotions are genuine and raw.

Although I won't know the names of the people who read this book, I will know one thing about them: that there is every chance they have been, or will be, a victim of Identity Theft. It is still the fastest-growing crime in the world, with one in ten people being affected by it in the UK alone. Even though, as in my case, you could end up losing everything, it is still considered to be a 'victimless crime'.

The book is divided into three sections;

1. Discovering my identity had been stolen and the distressing consequences.
2. Writing and performing a show about my experience and taking it to the Edinburgh Festival and beyond . . .
3. Making a television documentary to highlight the problem of Identity Theft, and subsequently being arrested in a dawn raid by Scotland Yard.

This is a true story. I just wish it weren't . . .

Part One

---

*It Wasn't Me,
It Was Bennett Arron*

Chapter 1

'And there's a school just around the corner . . . if you're planning on having children.'

My wife, Rosy, looked at me and smiled.

'Yes,' I said, 'that's the plan. Eventually.'

'And you said you've sorted out your mortgage?'

I nodded.

'Good. Well, if you have any questions or you'd like to have another viewing, just give me a call.'

The Estate Agent, in his double-breasted suit with turn-ups on the trousers, shook our hands, stepped into his spotless R-registration black BMW and drove off.

Rosy and I looked at the front of the house again. It really was ideal. Three bedrooms, detached, close to all amenities, situated in a pretty area of north London and with a school just around the corner. £175,000.

It was a lovely warm May afternoon in 1998. As Rosy and I drove back to the flat we were renting, less than a mile away from this house, we decided that we would put in an offer, fractionally under asking price, immediately.

I had been working as a stand-up comedian for just over a year. Although I wasn't making a living from it yet, this income, combined with money I was earning from writing sketches for radio and television, together with a small

1

sideline as a freelance printer, would be enough to cover the mortgage payments and put a little aside for the proverbial day of bad weather.

That night I had my seventieth stand-up gig. It was at the King's Head in Crouch End. Coincidentally that was the first proper venue I had ever really performed in as a comedian, almost eighteen months earlier. They have a New Act Night on a Thursday and it's where most of the current comics started.

To be honest, I'd never wanted to be a comedian. I'd always liked the idea of being a comedy performer – acting in sketches and sitcoms, etc. – but standing onstage on my own had never really appealed. In the late eighties I had started a comedy club called 'The Back of Beyond' in Cricklewood, north London. There weren't many clubs around at the time and the whole alternative circuit was still relatively new. I remember booking Paul Merton and Jo Brand for £30 a time. I also used to 'audition' newer comedians. They would perform five minutes of their set for me and I would then decide if they were good enough for my club! I remember telling one young hopeful that I couldn't book him as he just wasn't funny enough. His name was Eddie Izzard. In my defence, I wasn't the only one who thought he wasn't funny when he first started. I suppose he just hadn't yet found his 'voice'. I'd like to think his whole career has just been his way of proving me wrong.

One evening at the club, the compère hadn't turned up and the show was due to start. I therefore had to go on myself to warm up the audience. I was terrified. As I stood there mumbling incoherently, the compère arrived. I threw him the microphone and ran straight to the bar.

But here I was, ten years after running my own club, having a stand-up career of my own. At one of my early gigs I had been spotted by a talent scout for the BBC New Comedy Awards, who'd asked me if I would be interested in entering the competition. I was. So I did. I won all my heats and then went to the televised final in Edinburgh, where I was joint runner-up with Peter Kay. That's when I signed with an agent and began my life on the comedy circuit. And so far I was really enjoying it.

As I stood in the small dressing room along with the other comedians, waiting for our allotted stage time, I suddenly blurted out:

'I put an offer on a house today!'

I am, although I often deny it, a slightly superstitious person. It comes from my mother. My mother will never open an umbrella in the house ('unlucky'), never cross someone on stairs ('very unlucky') and never step over a child if they're lying on the floor ('they won't grow'). She also throws salt over her shoulder when she spills it. I used to laugh at this until once, when I was twelve, in the school canteen, I knocked over a salt cellar. I ignored it and then immediately proceeded to knock my tray into the tray of the school bully. Both the trays and I ended up smashed on the floor.

Apart from throwing salt, I am also a firm believer in not tempting fate. I never say something good is going to happen for fear of 'jinxing' it. However, I was so excited about buying the house I just couldn't help myself.

They all congratulated me, while throwing in comments like:

'That's all very grown-up.'

'You'll have 2.4 children next.'

And, 'I did a great corporate gig last night.'

Some comedians are quite self-obsessed.

As I drove back after the gig, I was working out how we'd organise the house. Because it had three bedrooms, we'd decided that one would be my office. I imagined having shelves all around with my superhero figures on them and, if there was enough space, some work files too.

Instead of going straight home, I drove to the house. I stopped the car outside and looked at it. I started wondering things like 'Which day do they collect the rubbish? What are the neighbours like?' I then saw myself in one if those sixties brightly coloured American suburban programmes, mowing the lawn and waving at neighbours.

'Yeah, ain't it a beautiful day.'

For one ridiculous fleeting moment I actually thought about naming the house. I quite liked 'Harold'.

The other thing I liked about this house was that it wasn't far from the place where I had first met Rosy. She had come to London from Spain to study English and was working as an au pair. I first saw her in the small corner shop where I bought my weekly groceries (if you can call pots of instant noodles and multipacks of crisps 'groceries'). I overheard her speaking to the shop owner and mentioning that she was from Spain. Once she left, I followed her outside, gave her my card and told her that if she ever wanted to see the sights of London to give me a call. I then ran off. Fortunately that night she rang me and we went out the following evening. How romantic – if not a tad stalkerish.

Our offer on the house was accepted and the following

couple of months were busy and exciting. We found a surveyor, engaged a solicitor, received quotes from removal firms, etc. I wrote to our landlord and gave notice on the flat we were renting. We were due to move in two months' time. Everything was falling into place. Everything for which we had worked so hard.

And then, at the last minute, it all changed.

Chapter 2

'Having carefully re-examined your application, I am sorry to tell you that it has not been agreed.'

'What?'

'Hang on, there's more . . . Your application was assessed using credit scoring . . . as part of the credit-scoring process an enquiry was made at a credit reference agency. The main reason for our decision was the reply we received.'

Rosy looked at me. 'What does that mean? The mortgage application was accepted months ago!'

'I know. I've no idea what this is. It's probably just a mistake.'

I looked at the letter in my hand.

If you wish to discuss any aspect of this letter, please feel free to contact me.

I turned to Rosy. 'As soon as I drop you off at work I'll give them a call.'

While Rosy went through her hair and make-up ritual, I flicked through the rest of the post; a late wedding-anniversary card, a utility bill and a royalty cheque for £7.50 for a television sketch I had written for Hale and Pace which had been shown in Australia.

I picked up the bank letter again. Credit scoring? I didn't know what that was. Surely it couldn't be anything to do with bad credit. I'd never been in debt. Ever. I'd always paid off my credit-card bills in full each month and never bought anything on hire purchase. Even when I was younger I'd always paid my monthly contributions to the Olivia Newton-John Fan Club on time – even though they never sent me the promised lock of hair. Or teeth.

After dropping Rosy off at work I stopped to get petrol. As I handed over my credit card and watched the grey machine slide over my card and the carbon papers, I thought about the letter again. Could anyone have used my credit card without my knowing? There had been nothing untoward on my last statement.

The moment I arrived back at the flat I called the bank. The manager knew me, as he was the one who had personally agreed the mortgage. I asked him if there had been a mistake. As I waited for him to look through the details I could hear myself pleading: please say 'yes', please say 'yes'.

'No, Mr Arron. There's no mistake.'

So much for the pleading. He told me that he didn't have much information, only that the mortgage had now been refused because of my outstanding debts. (I almost made a joke about whether he meant they were impressive.)

I told him that it couldn't be me as I wasn't in debt and never had been. I even explained the whole Olivia Newton-John thing.

He said that he appreciated my position but he couldn't do anything else. He explained that if I required further information I would have to contact a credit reference agency to obtain a credit report.

I said that I would do that immediately – once he'd explained what that meant.

After our conversation I looked at the notes I had written.

'Experian . . . Equifax . . . credit report . . . £2 . . .'

I apparently had to write to these companies, Experian and Equifax, send them £2 and request a credit report. This was something that would show me all my financial transactions and list any debts or creditors. It would also show me why my credit score was bad.

It didn't make any sense. I was still holding on to the belief that it was a mistake. I have an unusual name and very often people put it the wrong way around. Maybe there was someone with the name Arron Bennett who had a bad credit score. It was a thin straw, but I had to grab on to something.

I sent off the cheques.

Some Creationists believe that when the Bible states the world was created in six days it is not being literal and that each day is actually thousands if not millions of years. Waiting for those credit reports to arrive, I knew exactly what they meant. Everything was put on hold while we waited to see the information. It was all we could think about. Even watching an episode of ER couldn't take our minds off it.

Eventually the reports arrived. Once we read them, in a way we wished they hadn't. According to the reports, I owed thousands of pounds to various companies including a home shopping company, a mobile-phone company and a well-known large London department store. The thing was, I'd never bought anything from any of them.

It was genuinely awful seeing my name next to all these debts. And, even worse, I didn't know what to do about it. After reading through everything several times, I contacted the credit reference agencies and asked them what I should do. I explained that the debts were nothing to do with me and that I had to clear my name. They told me that the first thing I had to do was contact the police and report it as a crime.

I rang my local police station and that evening a police officer came to our flat. I told him exactly what had happened and showed him the bank letter and credit reports.

After listening to everything and making notes, the officer then turned to me and said, 'This is all very well and good, Mr Arron, but it's your name. So how do I know that it isn't really you yourself who has carried out the crime?'

'Yes, you're quite right officer,' I replied. 'It could be me. And perhaps I would have even got away with it – if I hadn't called you!'

After thinking about this for a while he told me that he would pass on the information to his superiors and that someone would get back to me.

The moment he left I turned to Rosy and said, 'It's true what they say – you know you're getting older when policemen are getting . . . thicker.'

Two days after the visit from PC Mensa, I received a telephone call from someone at the newly established Serious Fraud Office – they had obviously decided to bypass the Jocular one.

The officer asked me to go through the whole story again, which I did. After I'd finished, he said, 'You do realise, Mr Arron, that falsely claiming there's a fraud *is* a fraud.'

I thought if he tells me, 'And two wrongs don't make a right,' I'm going to hang up.

After further discussion, he somewhat begrudgingly gave me a case reference number. With my newly granted 'this is really a crime' code I wrote to the bank and the companies involved, explaining what had happened. I told them of the urgency of the situation and how I needed to clear my name as soon as possible. Then I waited. And waited. And waited.

Chapter 3

Dear Bennett, I'm afraid this material isn't up to your usual standard so we won't be able to use anything. If you'd like to send any more, please feel free to do so, but this will have to be on spec as we won't be able to commission any more work from you for the time being.

Not the type of post I had been hoping to receive that morning.

To be fair, this television producer had a point. With all that was going on, I was finding writing comedy a little difficult. Most of my recent sketches ended with people wanting to kill themselves.

For the previous three months I had been spending virtually all my time following up letters and phone calls to the various companies to which I didn't owe money and replying to letters and phone calls from debt collectors and lawyers.

I was still gigging occasionally and Rosy was working, but without the writing work and printing jobs, it wasn't enough on which to live. And I didn't have any time to look for new writing work or printing customers.

As no company had yet come back to me to clear my name, my credit rating was still zero. This prohibited me from doing many things; I couldn't open a new bank account, I couldn't get a new credit card and I couldn't take on a new mobile-phone contract. I couldn't even join my local gym as they wouldn't accept my direct debit – so it wasn't all bad news.

But of course, most importantly, the mortgage application was still being declined.

A couple of days after I received the letter from the television producer, I had a call from the estate agent. He told us that the vendors, understandably, couldn't wait for us indefinitely – so they were selling the house to someone else.

A few nights later, again on my way home from a gig, I drove past the house that should have been our new home. Seeing a SOLD sign outside was devastating.

The following day we contacted the landlord of the flat and explained that we needed to renew the contract for another six months. He apologetically told us that, as we had already given him notice, he'd let it to someone else.

We now had to quickly find somewhere else to live. Property prices were very low at that time and rents were high. When we'd taken out our rental contract we'd been given a great deal, which gave us the chance to save. Now, however, we'd have to pay almost double to rent somewhere else. Not to mention the deposit.

As my work, and therefore money, had declined, we had been dipping into our savings just for day-to-day expenses. We suddenly realised that our savings, including the 5% deposit we had saved for the house we had hoped to buy, had almost completely run out.

We didn't know what to do. I thought about looking for another job. But what could I do? After my A levels I had been accepted to study psychology at university. However, I had turned this down to attend drama school in London instead. I had been hoping that one day I would be a successful actor and my parents would then forgive me. I can't say I enjoyed drama school. In truth I found it a waste of time. I was therefore quite relieved when I was eventually kicked out.

So, I was thinking about looking for another job and . . . What? You'd like to know why I was kicked out of drama school? Okay, I'll briefly tell you . . .

As I mentioned, I found drama school a complete waste of time. Another person who found it a waste of time was the director of our end-of-year production. This production was a very big deal. Agents, casting directors and producers would be invited, alongside the obligatory family and friends of the cast. We were all very nervous and excited. The director however had no interest whatsoever. Before each rehearsal he would tell us how much he hated drama schools and drama students, how he should really be directing at the National Theatre and how he was only doing this directing job for the money.

One day when he was, as usual, late for rehearsal, we were all complaining about him. I suggested that one of us went to speak to the principal. Everyone agreed. Everyone then agreed that the person should be me. So I did. I went to her office and explained everything to her. She was genuinely shocked and upset to hear what I had to say. She then came back into the rehearsal room with me.

'Bennett has just told me that you're all very unhappy with the director,' she said. Everyone suddenly looked surprised. It was the best acting they had ever done or ever would do. 'No,' they said, almost as one 'That's not true.'

The principal looked at me. Not quite sure what to say, I apologised for wasting her time. Once she had left, my fellow cast members all came over to me and said that they were sorry but didn't want to cause a fuss. I smiled and told them to forget about it.

However, I wouldn't.

So, on the opening night of the play, when anyone who was anyone was there, I changed all my lines, ad-libbed and chatted with the audience. No one got their cue, so they didn't know when to come onstage. I had turned *Murder in the Cathedral* into a comedy, and the audience had loved it.

The principal and staff however had not been so keen. The next day I was given a letter suggesting that the type of thing I had done was not suitable for a drama school but more suited to a comedy club. It turned out to be the best piece of advice I'd been given the whole time I was there.

After leaving drama school I had taught drama for a while and then gave it up to be a full-time writer and actor. (I know!) Things hadn't been going too badly though. Until now.

Rosy and I considered our options. There weren't many. Then these suddenly became even more limited when we discovered that Rosy was pregnant. No, I don't know where I'd found the time either, but apparently I'd managed to fit it in . . . (I'm aware there's probably a better phrase than that!)

We were as happy as we were worried, but this wasn't how we'd hoped to start a family. We didn't know what to do. So, we decided that, as a temporary solution, just to save money and try to sort things out, we would move in with my parents in Wales. A Welsh production company had shown interest in a sitcom script I'd written, and I'd been to Cardiff for meetings with them. It looked like they were keen on going ahead so I thought they'd see my moving to Wales as a commitment to making the programme.

A couple of weeks later, with the majority of our stuff in storage, we drove a packed car to Wales, virtually crying all the way – and not just because of the toll charge on the Severn Bridge.

I don't know if you have ever lived with your partner and your parents, but if you have, you'll know how difficult it is. If you haven't, well, it's very difficult . . .

Living with your parents when you're a teenager can be tricky. Living with your parents as a married adult, with a wife who's pregnant and with very little money and the crime of Identity Theft hanging over you, is almost impossible.

Speaking of Identity Theft, we had decided not to tell my parents how serious the situation had become. I didn't want to worry them. Although they knew someone had been fraudulently using my name, as far as they were concerned, the main reason we had moved in was because of the programme in Cardiff. We had also decided not to tell them about the pregnancy yet. I suppose I'm quite traditional (or, as I mentioned earlier, superstitious) so I wanted to wait the customary three months before saying anything. However, it's different in Spain. There, the minute women know they're pregnant they tell virtually everyone. Sometimes they don't even wait that long – they ring their mum halfway through sex and say, 'I think this is it!'

But I wanted to wait, and Rosy agreed – without thinking of the consequences. For example, some mornings my mother would make breakfast, Rosy would take a mouthful and suddenly run off to be sick. It wasn't the best of compliments.

Even though I found living with my parents difficult, for Rosy, being pregnant and living with her in-laws was of course much harder. Having a Jewish mother and Spanish wife, both volatile, living under the same roof, isn't ideal – although it's probably the premise for a great sitcom.

There were some advantages to living in Wales however. For example, I had the opportunity of going to the synagogue with my father, which I hadn't done for quite a while. My parents' synagogue was actually the first place I had ever tried out some stand-up material.

I had been living in London for a while and had just started writing for television. I was at the time writing sketches for television programmes like *The Real McCoy* and *Hale and Pace* and occasionally I would come up with an idea or joke which wouldn't fit into a sketch so I would put it to one side. One day I looked through all these jokes and ideas and started working on a bit of a routine. I had no idea how funny it was, or in fact if it was funny at all. And I didn't know if I'd ever try it out.

An opportunity arose in May 1996. As I mentioned, I had left the stable career of teaching to pursue my dream of being a writer. I had decided, somewhat naively and dreamily, that the best place to do this would be Hollywood. I had always wanted to live in America, and Rosy, who loves travelling, needed very little persuasion. As we had nothing to tie us down we thought this would be the ideal time. So, with the help of family and friends, we left the UK and moved to Los Angeles – to live in view of the Hollywood sign. As well as trying to have meetings with agents and producers over there, I had plenty of time to continue working on my stand-up routine. There was a club on Sunset Boulevard, near where we lived, called the Comedy Store. It's where a number of great American comedians first started. I decided to ring the club and ask if they would allow a new act to try out material. They told me that I could have a slot at 2 a.m. I was delighted. Rosy on the other hand wasn't so keen. Although she's always supportive of every-thing I do, she really didn't like the thought of my being in what she saw as an unsafe area in the early hours of the morning. So I didn't do it. To be fair, she was probably right. Especially considering what happened, in front of family and friends in Wales, when I actually tried the material out for the first time . . .

Not long after returning from America I received a call from the chairman of the synagogue asking me if I would be one of their guest speakers at an anniversary celebration dinner. I thought this would now be a perfect opportunity to try out this material, especially as I would know the majority of the audience. So off I went to Wales. By train. On a Sunday. Needless to say there were delays, so I arrived late. I walked in and was told that I was to go on immediately. So I did my newly written eight minutes of comedy . . . to absolute silence. Nothing. I walked off, thinking to myself, 'Well, I tried. I will obviously never make it as a comedian.' The chairman then came up to me and apologised. They had all thought that I was going to talk about living in London and memories of the synagogue, etc. They hadn't realised that I was going to perform comedy. He explained that, had they known, they might not have given me a slot between a Holocaust survivor and the Chief Rabbi.

I decided then that no gig could ever go so badly. So far so good.

So now we were living in Wales. Under quite stressful conditions all round. Whilst we were there we had the first scan of the baby, which was of course very exciting, but also a little worrying when the midwife said, 'Ooh, you're lucky! Two for the price of one.'

She saw our shocked faces and then quickly followed this with, 'No, I don't mean twins. I mean we're doing an offer at the moment and you can have two copies of the scan photo for the price of one!'

We were quite relieved. And not only because we'd saved a pound.

I was still on the phone to companies every day or writing them letters – from my new 'c/o Mum and Dad' address – but no progress was being made.

I was also still gigging occasionally and obviously taking Rosy with me, mainly as I didn't want to leave her and my mum in the same house – my dad didn't deserve that.

It wasn't an ideal scenario and was a million miles away from the situation in which we had expected and hoped to be.

Rosy and I looked into the possibility of renting some-where in Wales as rental prices were substantially lower than London. We really weren't sure what to do. One evening we decided that we would go out for dinner and by the end of it we'd have made up our minds as to what our next actions should be.

However, by the end of the meal we still hadn't decided what to do – apart from not eating in that place again. We then left the restaurant to discover our car had been stolen. This might not be coming across, but we weren't having the best of times.

So we looked upon this as a sign (or, in truth, just a reason) for us not to stay in Wales any longer. The thing was, I knew Rosy was missing her family. They were obviously aware that we were living with my parents, but they thought it was just to save money. They didn't know the whole story. Rosy hadn't told them about the Identity Theft or, against custom, about the pregnancy. She wanted to tell them everything face to face.

So, after telling my parents about the baby (it was now close enough to three months), we packed our maximum baggage allowance and flew to Spain.

Chapter 4

The first few of days living in Spain were, unsurprisingly, quite emotional. As Rosy's parents didn't know what had been going on, you can imagine their surprise when they heard those words all parents want to hear from their only daughter:

'I'm pregnant and homeless.'

Rosy explained everything to them. Well, as far as I know she did. Her parents don't speak a word of English and I speak Spanish like a native. Of Hungary.

What should have been a wonderful, celebratory time was instead a depressing one. The thought that someone had done this to us made me incredibly angry. Going for a walk on my own one evening, I vowed to myself that I would somehow, one day, track down the person responsible.

We had our second scan in Spain and thankfully everything was still okay with the baby – although this time, unfortunately, we only received one copy for our money.

I was obviously still contacting the banks and companies etc, but doing it from Spain was very difficult. I was constantly put on hold, so the calls were very expensive. And as there was no point in having my post redirected to Spain, my dad said he'd call me if anything important arrived. So far nothing had.

As in Wales, we thought about staying and having the baby there. I even went to see some agencies that booked comedians for hotels. However, even though the majority of guests at these hotels were English, they wanted someone who could also perform in Spanish and French. Without changing all my material to jokes where the only words were 'Yes', 'No', 'How are you?' and 'Beer', this wouldn't be me.

After two months in Spain, and with no progress on anything, I realised that I would have to come back to the UK to sort things out. Not only did I need to clear my name, but I also needed to work.

So, leaving Rosy with her family, I flew back to London.

For the next few days I stayed with friends, borrowed their cars and looked for somewhere, anywhere, that was cheap enough for us to rent. It was so upsetting. There was one particular day in January 1999, which I will never forget. It was 4.30 p.m., pitch black, windy and pouring with rain. I'd been driving around for most of the day looking at one flat after another, each in a worse condition than the last. I pulled over to the side of the road and thought to myself, 'I'm sleeping on a friend's floor, driving a borrowed car, desperately trying to find somewhere to live while my wife is hundreds of miles away pregnant with our first child. This was not how I expected my life to pan out.' I then burst into tears.

Eventually, after more days of looking, I found somewhere just outside London. I told Rosy and we made arrangements for her to leave Spain. As you can imagine, the prospect of leaving her parents, not knowing what was going to happen next, was incredibly stressful and harrowing – not the best situation to be in when you're pregnant. However we both wanted to be together, and we knew I couldn't work there.

Not long after we moved into our new place, friends of ours won a car in a competition. As they didn't drive, they very kindly sold it to us at a reduced price – and even allowed us to pay in instalments.

Now that we'd moved once more, I had to contact all the companies again and give them yet another address.

Slowly, over the next few weeks, because of my persistent calling and writing, I eventually started to receive responses from some of the companies involved with the fraud. Some wanted more information, while others just stated that, as the accounts were in my name, I was obviously accountable for the debts. The main problem was that no one had really heard about Identity Theft so they assumed I was just trying some sort of con. One of the companies, a mobile-phone operator, told me that according to their records there were two accounts in my name. They informed me that one of the accounts had been stopped, as I still owed a substantial amount of money on it. I interrupted and explained that it wasn't me and that someone was fraudulently using my name. They then told me that the other account was still up and running but that as I owed money on that one too, it would also be stopped unless I paid in full. I explained, again, that it wasn't me and that someone was fraudulently using my name. They had no interest in this; they just wanted their money.

I asked for number on the account that was still up and running.

'You have it,' they said. 'It's your number!'

I explained, again, that it wasn't me and that someone was fraudulently using my name. I could almost hear them shrugging their shoulders. I then asked them to just humour me and give me the number. Which they eventually did.

So I rang the number and someone answered.

'Hello,' I said. 'Is that Bennett Arron?'

This is something I've heard many times on the phone but had never actually said myself.

'Yes!' said the voice on the other end.

This really threw me, mainly because this person was curt and abrupt whereas I'm always really polite on the phone.

I then said, 'Snap!'

There was a brief pause and then the line went dead.

I rang back but it went straight to voicemail. And it wasn't my voice.

It was really weird. I had spoken with the person who had stolen my identity. The person who was responsible for our situation. Rosy could see that I was shaken by the call.

I waited for an hour or so, mainly to compose myself, and then rang the mobile-phone company again. I asked them if they would send me a copy of the contract which had been taken out in my name. After telling me that surely I must have a copy myself, as I was the one who took it out, they eventually informed me that the account had been opened at an independent phone shop in Whetstone, north London. They would have the contract.

So that afternoon I went to the shop and spoke with the owner. I explained that two accounts had been fraudulently opened in my name from his shop and that I needed a copy of the contract(s) as I was trying to find out as much information as possible to ascertain who had carried out the crime.

After I'd finished my explanation he just stood there, staring at me. I wasn't sure if he'd misheard or misunderstood. Maybe it was the word 'ascertain' that was causing the problem.

He then took a step closer to me and said, 'Get out of my shop! If you don't get out, now, I'll call my mates and they'll come here and make sure you get out!'

I knew he wasn't lying – he had loads of phones.

So, shocked and shaken, I left the shop and went home. I immediately rang the mobile-phone company and told them what had happened. At first they didn't seem to believe me – for a change. I then questioned them on why they themselves wouldn't have a copy of the contract. Surely, even though the phone had been issued by an independent store, they must have been sent a copy of the contract to register my account with their network.

They agreed.

I asked them if they would therefore send me a copy of that contract.

They agreed.

Two weeks later, I had still not received anything. I rang and asked why it hadn't been sent.

'We're very sorry, Mr Arron. We did find your contract. However, before we'd had the chance to send it to you, we lost it.'

'Er . . . pardon?'

'We lost it. We've looked everywhere but we can't seem to find it.'

It's not often I'm speechless. Even if it's something not quote-worthy I am usually able to offer up some kind of verbal retort. But not this time. I simply hung up the phone, looked at the address on their letterhead and drove to their offices in Borehamwood, Hertfordshire.

Once there, I explained to the receptionist what had happened and told her that I would not leave until I was given a copy of the contract. She threatened to call the police. I gave her the number of my contact at the Serious Fraud Office. She then disappeared. Moments later she returned with a copy of the contract. And charged me ten pence for it.

As I've mentioned, I have quite an unusual name and people often think I'm called Arron Bennett. I'm not. This is obviously what happened when the contract had been filled out. The person in the shop had originally written my name as Arron Bennett and then crossed it out and made the correction. It's funny to imagine the fraudster getting annoyed when he saw 'his' name the wrong way around. By the way, I hate the term 'fraudster'. I know it's the term used by the police, but to me it sounds too glamorous. The correct term is 'thief' or 'criminal'.

This criminal actually did quite well on the mobile phone deal! I'm not sure if I could have done better myself. The contract required my date of birth. However, as he didn't know it… he just made one up. And it was never challenged. (He did at least make me a little younger, so he's not all bad.)

The contract showed an address where I'd lived prior to being married – which was now four addresses ago! I checked this address with the information from the credit reference agencies. The majority of the bad credit had come from there.

I immediately contacted my old landlord and asked if he had rented the flat out to someone after me. He told me that after I had moved out he had actually sold the property – I didn't take it personally. He gave me the number of the new owner, who he said was a friend of his. I rang this new owner and explained the situation. This new owner told me that he too had rented the flat out. Just the once. The tenant had stayed for six months, paid only one month's rent, trashed the place and eventually moved on. He gave me the person's name. This name had come up several times on my credit report as it cross-referenced the electoral register from this previous address. Now, I was no Helen Mirren, but I believed I had my Prime Suspect.

I rang my contact at the Serious Fraud Office and gave him all the information I had been given by the owner of the property. The Serious Fraud Officer actually knew of this ex-tenant! Apparently he was part of a Nigerian fraud ring and they had been chasing him for quite a while but to no avail. I told him if I found out anything more, I would let him know.

After hanging up, I thought about this. Could I find out anything else about this person? As I had managed to uncover some details from the mobile-phone account, I wondered if there were other accounts that might still be up and running in my name from which I could extract further information. So I looked at all the companies on the credit report and rang their customer services departments, this time asking about active accounts.

The home shopping company told me that there was an

account running within a division of their group. I explained the whole situation to them. We then had the following conversation:

Me: 'So the account is definitely an active account, that is still up and running?'
Them: 'Yes, Mr Arron.'
Me: 'Is there an address on this account?'
Them: 'Yes, Mr Arron.'
Me: 'Would you give me that address, please?'
Them: 'No, Mr Arron.'
Me: 'Sorry?'
Them: 'No, we won't give you the address.'
Me: 'Er . . . why?'
Them: 'Because you have just explained that this person isn't you. So we can't give you their details.'

I opened and closed my mouth a few times. I wasn't sure how to start the next sentence and was surprised that I even had to. I tried to hold back my irritation and not sound patronising.

Me: 'Yes. I fully understand that this person isn't me. However, this person has stolen my identity and is pretending to be me . . .'
Them: 'Therefore, you are not this person. And, under the Data Protection Act we cannot give you someone else's information.'

No, they weren't kidding. I really didn't know how to respond. So I simply thanked them for their 'help' and hung up.

An hour later – and I think this is one of the best things I've ever done – I rang them back. This time I pretended I was me, and asked them where I lived.

And they told me.

I had moved to a flat near Paddington, so I was obviously doing quite well for myself.

That evening, Rosy and I drove to the address I'd been given – and she says I never take her anywhere! There were no lights on in the flat so we sat in the car and waited for the person who had stolen my identity to return home. After about an hour, just as we were finishing our sandwiches and the last drop of soup from the flask, we saw the thief – who had been described to us by his previous landlord – walking to the front door.

I'll be honest; I didn't know what to do. I hadn't thought much beyond this point. Looking at him, part of me just wanted to go up and punch him. But I didn't. And the only reason I didn't, the ONLY reason, was because . . . he was huge!

It was a really odd feeling, watching the person who had stolen my identity, the person who had caused me to lose everything, just walking in front of me. Strangely, and I don't know why, but the fact he looked nothing like me annoyed me even more. I know it doesn't make sense, but had he been a short, stocky, balding Jewish/Welsh guy, I might have accepted it a bit more. But he wasn't.

I looked at Rosy.

'Come on,' she said. 'Let's go back.'

I only wished we could.

Chapter 5

Yasmin.

It was the only name we'd agreed on, so it was fortunate she was a girl. But she was a girl. A beautiful, wonderful, adorable girl. And I know that every father says their daughter is the most beautiful girl in the word, but they're wrong. Although, to be honest with you, with everything that had been going on, I was half expecting her to be Nigerian . . .

The morning after seeing the criminal walk into his flat in Paddington I had contacted the Serious Fraud Office and given them the address. They were surprised by the information I'd acquired and thanked me for tracking him down. I explained that I was just 'doing my job'. I told them that I wanted to be told when the case went to court, as I would obviously want to be a witness. In truth I wanted to go on the Witness Protection Scheme and get a new identity.

So I had done as much as I could. I had tracked down the person who had stolen my identity, and handed him over to the police. It was now time to concentrate on our new addition to the family – born a month after our picnic at Paddington – and try to put our lives back into some sort of shape.

Over the next few months, I slowly started to receive letters from almost all the banks, companies and debt-collection agencies, reluctantly accepting that the debts were not mine and that I wasn't being held responsible. Unfortunately, if not too little, it certainly was too late.

Money was still quite tight. Although I had started working more and I was slowly beginning to make a little bit of a name for myself on the comedy circuit, having just had a baby meant I didn't really want to be touring around the country, spending time away from home. I had managed to pick up a couple of small writing jobs and was also writing material for other comedians. However, even with this income, we were unable to buy a property. The house we had wanted to buy at £175,000 had now doubled in price. Doubled! Because of the thief, we had missed the opportunity to buy a house at the best time, and now we didn't know when, or if, we ever would.

A couple of months after Yasmin had been born, and our sleep patterns fortunately had become more regular, I started thinking about what had happened over the past year. Incredibly, with all that had been going on, there was one important question which hadn't been answered: How did he do it?! How had this thief managed to take over my life and ruin it? I had no idea. And I wanted to find out.

I once again contacted all the companies involved – they were delighted to hear from me – and asked them what proof of identity had been used to open the accounts in my name. You won't be surprised to learn that they weren't too forthcoming with the information. However, I persevered and, eventually, after consistent letters and phone calls, I discovered what had happened. And to this day I still can't believe how easy it was . . .

The home shopping company had sent out mailshots asking people if they would like a catalogue. Even though I'd had my post redirected, one of these mailshots had slipped through and been sent to my old address. (I'm not sure why my name was on their database, I assume it was from the electoral register). The thief, now living at this address, had replied to this mailshot saying that yes, 'I' would like a catalogue. He had then been sent one along with an order form. He had ordered something and they had sent him the item (I'm not sure what it was, but I'm guessing it wouldn't have been my size), together with the new account information – set up in my name. Simply, with this new proof of account, he had gone to the mobile-phone shop in north London and asked for a phone. I assume that the then-pleasant owner of the shop had said something like, 'Sure, why not have two?' And then set up the phone account(s). Now, with more 'proof' of identity, he had applied for, and received, a store credit card. He then applied for other credit cards and opened other accounts, each time building up more and more fake ID. That is how it had happened. That easily.

As you can imagine, when I discovered the ease with which the thief had managed to carry out this fraud, I was furious. This had not been my fault in any way. The companies had all allowed this to happen.

I contacted each company involved again and told them how I had lost everything because of their negligence and that I now wanted compensation. Each one in turn wrote back and agreed that they were to blame and asked me how much I wanted.

I'm kidding.

Each company told me how they had 'acted in good faith' when they had received the applications. Oh, well, that's okay then. Sorry to have bothered you.

I spoke with a representative at the home shopping company, who informed me that, as quite a few people had suffered problems as a result of these mailshots, they had cut back on the number they sent out. Two weeks after this conversation – they sent me a mailshot! They had taken my address from my private correspondence and added me to their mailing list! When I contacted them and told them this, they told me it was a coincidence. A coincidence! I realised it was pointless pursuing anything with this company so I gave up.

The next company I contacted in the hope of some kind of justice was the mobile-phone company that had allowed accounts to be opened with simply a catalogue bill as proof of identity. Over the next few months more than fifty letters went back and forth between us. One of their letters would state that, although they did not accept culpability, they would look into my compensation claim. The following letter would state that they had spoken to their lawyers and they were not going to pay me anything. This went on and on. During our exchange of correspondence they changed managing director twice. I hoped that was because of me. Eventually they simply stopped replying to my letters or answering my phone calls, so I had to give up on this too.

The same thing happened with each of the other companies I pursued. Even though they accepted that I wasn't culpable, they insisted that they weren't either. The loss department from one of the major department stores said to me, 'We're all victims in this.' Yes, except that their losses were minimal whereas mine had affected my life. This same department store actually suggested I should contact the police about it and report it as a crime. Brilliant idea. Only I had already done that, and they had a copy of the police report!

Now you might be wondering what was actually going on with the police while all this was happening. Was the thief on bail awaiting trial? Was he already in prison? I had no idea. I had contacted the Serious Fraud Office on several occasions but no one could, or would, tell me what was happening.

Eventually, weeks later, after several phone calls, I did manage to speak to someone – but it wasn't the conversation I'd expected.

The officer with whom I spoke sounded very uncomfortable as he explained to me what had happened. Incredibly, even though I had given the police the name, address and description of the person who had stolen my identity, they had not gone to the property immediately to arrest him. In fact they had waited over six months to follow it up. By which time, he had moved on and they'd lost track of him.

That was that.

I then made the decision to give up on the whole thing, put it all behind me and move on with my life.

So I did.

Until six years later . . .

Chapter 6

'…The Comic and the Cloned ID…'. Here I was on the inside pages of a newspaper. A large double-page spread. (I'm sure they'd thought about putting me on page three, but wondered how many car mechanics would stick the photo of a stocky, hairy, topless man on their wall.) Seven years after having my identity stolen, and six years, to the day, since Yasmin had been born, I was a major story in a national newspaper.

Michael, my closest friend and one of the first people I met when I moved to London, works in advertising. One of his agency's clients, a credit-card company, was bringing out a product which was intended to help with ID theft. Their PR people wanted to speak with anyone who'd had personal experience of the crime. So, after checking that I didn't mind, Michael put them in touch with me.

It was strange talking about it again. Even though of course I hadn't forgotten what had happened, it was something I had tried to put to the back of my mind. Now, speaking about it again, all the emotions of hurt, stress and anger returned.

After I'd finished telling my story, the interviewer told me that she had spoken to over a hundred people who had been affected by the crime and my story was the worst. Although I am quite a competitive person I wasn't happy about winning this. She then asked me if I would be willing to speak to the press about my experience.

When I first went to drama school – and was subsequently expelled – I had wanted to be a 'bit famous' and see my photo in the newspaper. However, to be honest, I was hoping to be discussing how I had won a small golden bald statue instead of explaining how I had lost everything to a thief. Still, believing the old adage about publicity, I agreed, hoping in some way to try and turn this to my advantage.

In the interview for the paper, the journalist had asked me if I spoke about the Identity Theft in my stand-up set. I explained that I didn't mention it as I thought there would be little interest. However, they pointed out that the subject was now in the news a lot more – especially as Alistair McGowan, the face of the Capital One ad campaign, had had his identity stolen by a tabloid newspaper – so I was possibly wrong.

After the piece had been published, I thought more about this. I realised that putting the subject into my normal stand-up set would be odd and probably a bit pointless. I couldn't imagine, for example, performing a late-night show to stag and hen nights and suddenly stopping my usual gag-based routine to tell them about the ease and consequences of Identity Theft: 'Hey, kids, when you've finished shouting things out and throwing drinks over each other, don't forget to shred your documents!' So I decided to write a one-man show on the subject. I don't know why – it was probably for some cathartic reason – but from the moment I started writing it, I couldn't stop.

By this point, in 2005, I had been a comedian for around nine years. In addition to our beautiful daughter, we now also had a wonderful son, who had been born at the end of December 2002. We had named him Xander, after Rosy had bluntly rejected my suggestions of Troy or Wolverine.

Since Xander's birth, as well as gigging, I'd written for a couple of television programmes and had a sitcom script optioned by the BBC, paid for by the BBC, read through for the BBC and then turned down by the BBC. I'd also been running some comedy-writing workshops – those who can, etc. But now I was working on a solo stand-up show.

Over the years I had worked hard on my stand-up routines and they had taken me a long time to write and rewrite. However this, my first ever one-man show, took very little time. Of course it was a true story and I wasn't simply looking for jokes or embellishing stories. Obviously I was still trying to make it funny, and I found that most of the humour was fortunately/unfortunately already there. From the officer coming to my house to interview me, to my calling the home shopping company and pretending I was 'me'; the situations, which were far from amusing at the time, were now cast in a new light.

I loved writing the show and I finished a first draft of the whole thing in two weeks. I had never done that before – or since.

So I had a show. But would I ever perform it? And if so, where? And, more importantly, if I did ever put it on, would anyone excluding close family and friends, be at all interested? I had once performed a sketch show at the Etcetera Theatre, a small but perfectly formed space above the Oxford Arms pub in Camden High Street. I contacted the girls who ran the theatre and asked if they had a gap. They had. There was an hour free, on three consecutive nights, ahead of a show being performed by my friend Robin Ince. Robin had been very good to me when I first started as a stand-up and had recommended me to several venues and promoters so I really liked the idea of doing my show on the same nights as his.

For the next couple of weeks I walked around the area where I live, rehearsing my routine and trying to remember it. I was as excited about the show as I was worried. Standing onstage on your own for twenty minutes can be nerve-wracking at times; the thought of doing it for an hour, with all new, untried material, was perturbing to say the least.

Of course, as Rosy kept telling me when she could see how nervous I was, no one was forcing me to do this. It was my choice. Yet I really wanted to do it. And, as with stand-up when I first started, I had decided to just do the three nights and see how it went.

So, in June 2005, I performed my first ever one-man show.

It didn't go well.

There were very few people in the audience, and those few were made up of Rosy, the agents who looked after my television writing work, a couple of good friends and two girls from the pub downstairs who were early for Robin's show. However, I had gone through the whole thing, keeping to the script, and not succumbing to my gut

37

reaction of going into old, tried and tested material just to get laughs. It was very difficult for me to judge what, if any of it, was funny.

On the way home, I wasn't in the best of moods. Apart from anything else, the show had lasted forty-five minutes rather than an hour. I couldn't kid myself that, had the room been full and the show good, laughter would have added another fifteen minutes.

That night I stayed up until the early hours, rewriting the parts I felt could have worked better. Part of me wanted to cancel the following two nights, but I had promised myself, and of course the theatre, that I would do all three. And, more importantly, I'd paid for it.

Fortunately the second night was busier, and better. It was also very interesting, as I'd invited representatives from the credit reference agency Experian to come and watch. They really enjoyed it – especially when I mentioned that they were one of the companies I'd contacted when I had my identity stolen.

That night the journey home was much better. I still stayed up until late rewriting the parts that hadn't worked as well as I had hoped, but there wasn't as much work as the previous night.

The third and final show was, as one would hope, the best of the three. Bigger audience, bigger laughs and thankfully almost an hour long. There were also some more people from Experian in the audience. They had been told about it by their colleagues and had come along to see it for themselves.

I came away from the whole thing feeling very pleased with myself. I had written a show about my personal experience and, on two of the three nights, made people laugh. Intentionally. Of course not all the show was meant to be comedic. There were serious and very emotional moments, especially when I relived the moment of Rosy being in Spain, pregnant with Yasmin, while I tried to find somewhere for us to live.

Still, I had done it and I was proud of myself. I didn't know if I'd ever perform the material again, but that was fine. I had achieved what I had set out to do.

Two weeks after the final show, the girls from the Etcetera Theatre rang me and told me that a friend of theirs, who was running a new venue at the Edinburgh Festival, had a last-minute cancellation and was now looking for a show to fill a ten-day gap. They had very nicely mentioned my show to him and he sounded keen.

My immediate reaction was to thank them for thinking of me but to decline. Doing my own little intimate show in a small theatre in London was one thing, but taking it to the Edinburgh Festival, having only performed it three times, was not something that appealed. The girls however insisted it would work really well and told me to think about it before making any definite decision.

Even though I was pretty sure I'd made up my mind, that evening I chatted about it with Rosy. We weighed up the potential pros and cons.

Pros:
- It could do well and raise my profile. I could potentially make money from it.

Cons:

- As it was all so last minute I wouldn't be able to advertise in the overpriced but necessary Fringe Programme.
- Things were financially quite tight so I couldn't really pay for accommodation/PR/advertising etc.
- I would be away from Rosy and the children for ten days.

The cons outweighed the pros quite considerably.

So although the idea did, in a slight way, appeal, it was offset by the practicalities.

That night, lying in bed, I had an idea. What if I could find a sponsor for the show? I didn't know if that were feasible or if it was the done thing, but if I could find someone to pay for at least some of the costs, then the pros could equal the cons.

The fact that I was even thinking about this made me realise that I did actually want to do it. Whatever my gut reaction had been, part of me was happy with the show and felt that perhaps it was good enough to take to the festival.

The following morning I wrote to Experian and asked them if they would be interested in sponsoring me. In return, I explained, I would have their name on all my leaflets and posters and mention them in the show and in any interviews I did to promote the show. (I assumed that if they sponsored me, their own PR department could work on the show and benefit us both.)

They agreed!

So I booked plane tickets for Rosy and the children to

go to Spain to stay with Rosy's parents. I also booked tickets for me to join them eleven days later. I would be there in time to celebrate our tenth wedding anniversary.

Or so I thought.

Chapter 7

So the fourth performance of my first ever one-man show, entitled *It Wasn't Me, It Was Bennett Arron* was to be performed at the Edinburgh Festival. Unfortunately however it wasn't performed on what was scheduled to be the opening night. Or the following night. Due to low audience numbers – zero – the first two shows had to be cancelled. The problem was, no one knew the show was on! The Experian PR team had, as I had hoped, been working on publicising the show and I had a team to give out flyers for me. I had also contacted the press to let them know about the show, as it had an 'angle' I thought they might find interesting. But this was all going to take time. On the third evening I did eventually perform the show. To two people. As it so happens they both really enjoyed it, and I enjoyed performing it, and we had a chat about it afterwards. I had another week to go in Edinburgh and I couldn't wait to leave and join Rosy and the children in Spain. I had many friends who were also performing at the festival but, unlike the last time I had gone there, when I was part of a four-man show, I wasn't socialising very much. I was up early every morning to go to a cyber-café to write to all the newspapers and local radio stations to try to drum up interest in the show. I was there at 9 a.m. and left at 4 p.m. to prepare for the show. It was tiring and a little soul-destroying. Edinburgh is a tough place at the best of times and people have lost thousands of pounds by taking a show there – usually at the behest of their management company. Of course it can, and does, make people's careers too. But unfortunately the successes are dwarfed by the failures.

By the seventh day of my ten-day run, slight word-of-mouth together with other publicity meant that the audience numbers had increased a little. However, I was in a room which could hold more than 200 and I was having audiences of around ten to fifteen.

Unbeknown to me, there had been two critics at one of the performances. I only found out when someone from Experian rang me to congratulate me on my reviews. Both critics had written fantastic pieces, given me four stars and recommended my show as a 'must-see'. Suddenly the audience numbers dramatically increased. The show on the 8th night was the best I had done so far. It was fantastic having such great feedback – and the bits I had been adding and changing were now working really well.

The following day the venue organiser, the person who had booked me in the first place, called me for a meeting in his office. He told me that the theatre space in which I was performing was now free until the end of the Edinburgh Festival and he asked me, because of the good reviews and increased interest, if I wanted to extend my run. I immediately declined. He suggested I wait for that night – which would be my penultimate show – before making any definite decision. I was pretty sure I wasn't going to change my mind. The thought of staying an extra two weeks filled me with dread, and not just because I wouldn't see Rosy and the children and I would miss our anniversary. It was just too much. Too stressful. Too hard. No, there was no way I was going to do it.

After that penultimate show, which was incredible, I rang Rosy and asked her how she'd feel about celebrating our anniversary two weeks after the event. As always she was understanding and supportive. She had been delighted about the reviews and knew this could potentially lead to something very good.

The next day I cancelled my flight to Spain and then contacted Experian to ask them if they would finance the show for another two weeks. Unfortunately, although they had been incredibly generous from the outset, they explained that they didn't have the budget to do this. The accommodation they had organised for me had obviously only been booked for the ten days too, so I had to find somewhere else.

Acquiring accommodation in Edinburgh during the festival is almost impossible. In the same way as every room above or below a pub becomes a venue, so every available flat and house becomes an overpriced temporary home for as many people as it can hold. And then a couple more.

Fortunately my friend Julia, who books comedy clubs and knows many people in Edinburgh, told me that a friend of hers had a spare room in her flat for the remainder of the festival – at a good price. It was a bus journey from the city centre, but I was in no position to be fussy or complain. So I moved in.

I had contacted the press over the fact that my run had been extended – and made a point of mentioning that I wouldn't be with my wife on our anniversary. Fortunately they were interested – the human-interest angle – and incredibly the story ran on the homepage of the BBC website!

During this time I had been commissioned to write episodes of a children's television series, Genie in the House. So, now that there was nothing more to tell the press, I spent my mornings writing. Knowing my show was going well was a very relaxing feeling and helped with the writing.

I had worked hard and had been incredibly stressed, but now I had decided that I would try to enjoy the rest of the run. My brother came up to visit, as did my friend Michael, and I socialised a lot more. The Edinburgh Festival can be an incredible experience. You can, if you so desire, find somewhere to drink twenty-four hours a day. As a comedian you are running on adrenalin the whole time, and you can easily find a gig to perform at until the early hours of the morning. That's why so many comedians are ill the moment they come back from Edinburgh – the body is catching up with the late nights, lack of sleep, irregular eating patterns and, of course, alcohol consumption. It's like one month-long night out followed by one month-long hangover.

During my last week at the festival I received a phone call from someone in Italy. The caller, Fabio, explained that he was organising speakers for a 'Fraud and Identity Theft' conference in Rome in two months' time. He'd heard about my show and wanted to know if I would be interested in speaking at the event and if so, what my fee would be.

He'd heard about my show. In Italy!

As a comedian you are sometimes asked to perform at 'corporate gigs' – as well as the odd wedding, birthday, bar-mitzvah, etc. These can be very lucrative, although also, at times, quite awful. Even though I had performed at many of these corporate gigs, I had never been invited to perform at one abroad. I didn't know what fee to ask, and I had no agent to advise me. Also, having been away from the family for so long, I didn't like the thought of leaving them again. So, after thinking about it for a while, I rang Fabio back and told him that my fee would be flights and accommodation for myself, Rosy and the children, together with a bit of spending money. He told me that he would run it past the committee and get back to me.

I knew that Rosy had always wanted to visit Rome and, as the conference in Italy was taking place during half-term, Yasmin, now six, wouldn't have to miss school. So I was really hoping they would agree to my terms. Fortunately they did. I immediately rang Rosy and told her. She was incredibly excited and started planning what she would pack to take with her.

By the end of the festival, even though I was emotionally and physically exhausted, I was delighted with the 'buzz' the show had eventually received. And of course the fact we were going to Rome meant that something good had come out of it.

Unfortunately the next thing to come out of it wasn't so good . . .

Part Two

How To Steal An Identity

Chapter 8

A week after I returned home from the festival, my friend Julia contacted me to ask if I would be interested in speaking with a production company to discuss the possibility of turning my show into a television programme. She had to repeat this three times before it sank in. A friend of hers was a producer at a company which made factual television programmes. They wanted to pitch some new ideas to Channel 4 under its New Directors Scheme and were looking for unique and interesting ideas. Julia had mentioned my show to them and they liked the idea. So I had a meeting with Sally, one of the producers at the production company, and we worked on a way of pitching it to Channel 4. It would be an hour-long documentary which would include my Edinburgh show, intercut with my carrying out stunts to show how easy it is to steal someone's identity. I loved the idea of doing it, especially as, on top of everything else, I would be the director.

I'd always wanted to be a director, ever since I used my dad's old Super 8 camera to film my brother pretending he was the Six Million Dollar Man. So this was potentially a fantastic opportunity. All I had to do was pitch my idea – against those of all the other hopeful candidates – to Rebecca, one of the executives at Channel 4. For the next few weeks I worked on the proposal with Sally and her team. My main objective, as well as making the programme interesting and entertaining, was to make it funny. Sally had never dealt with comedy before so it was difficult explaining why I wanted to do or say certain things in a certain way.

The day arrived for the pitch and I was put into a room with the other would-be directors, all of whom would be pitching in turn to Rebecca. I had worked out exactly what I was going to say and had learned it off by heart – I didn't want to read a script. However, just before Rebecca came into the room I had an idea. I turned to one of the other candidates and asked him if he would start my pitch for me. He looked bemused. I explained that, if he didn't mind, I would like him to say; 'Hello, my name is Bennett Arron and my documentary is on the subject of Identity Theft.' The other candidate agreed – just as the door opened and Rebecca walked in. We went around the table pitching our ideas. Fortunately the person I had asked to introduce mine was speaking before me. Had he not been, my idea wouldn't have worked.

'Hello,' he said, 'my name is Bennett Arron and my documentary is on the subject of Identity Theft . . .' I then immediately interjected with; 'No! I'M Bennett Arron and MY documentary is on the subject of Identity Theft!'

There was a long, uncomfortable silence. No one knew what was going on. I left this as long as I felt I could and then continued with, 'Identity Theft is the fastest-growing crime in the UK. It happened to me once – and almost just happened to me again.'

There was relief in the room as everyone – well, almost everyone – realised what I had done.

My pitch seemed to go well and we were all told that we would hear the following week if we'd been successful. I'm by nature a pessimistic person so I'd already decided mine wouldn't be chosen. Still, I was pleased with my pitch and even thought about pitching it to other broadcasters – or trying to make the film myself.

I had returned to performing 'normal' gigs. It was weird doing this after my run at the Edinburgh Festival. In Edinburgh people had come to see me, personally. They had made a decision to spend their time and money on seeing my solo show. Now, back at regular comedy clubs, I was just one of several unknown names in a line-up for which people had either bought tickets just to see comedy, regardless of who was on, or because they were part of a group night out and therefore had little choice in going.

Although I'd received good reviews for my show, one of the criticisms I'd had was that I had used a flip chart to show the correspondence I had received from the various companies. Even though I had obviously enlarged the letters, etc, it was still quite a weak, basic way of presenting. I had therefore decided that, for Italy, I would put the letters into a PowerPoint presentation. I had sent this to the IT team in Rome in advance. They in turn had translated it all into Italian. I know it sounds obvious, but this was the first time it had dawned on me that I would be performing for people who might not speak English. As they hadn't asked me to learn Italian for the show I assumed they would have some means of translating. Otherwise I was going to receive as much of a response as at the cancelled shows in Edinburgh.

'Congratulations, yours has been chosen.'

'Sorry?'

'They've chosen yours as one of the programmes for the series!'

Sally sounded genuinely excited.

'Really?!' I said. 'That's fantastic!'

'I know. It's going to be a lot of work as yours is one of the most difficult ones to organise, but it's going to be great!'

I put the phone down and turned to Rosy to tell her. However she'd already guessed from my side of the conversation. She hugged me and said how she hoped this would be the turning point. The start of something great.

The schedule for making the programme was really intense – especially for a first-time director. I would be in the production-company offices in central London most days, researching and planning the scenes I wanted to shoot. Although my Edinburgh show would be the backbone of the piece, I planned to interview other major victims of Identity Fraud and representatives from Experian and the police. I also wanted to speak to the managing directors of the companies that had allowed my identity to be stolen in the first place. But before all this, I would have to learn how to direct . . .

I was initially given a crash course in how to use a broadcast-quality TV camera. Although I would have a cameraman with me on the main shoot, my trip to Rome for the fraud conference was coming up and, while there, I wanted to interview two people on camera. These were

Fabio, who had initially booked me for the conference and who was a Qualified Fraud Examiner, and Tom Craig who was also speaking at the conference and who, by incredible coincidence, had been the Head of Fraud at Scotland Yard when I had my identity stolen!

When I had pitched the idea of the programme, I had said that I planned to steal the identity of someone, just to show how easy a crime it was to carry out. I had thought it would be fun, and ironic, to steal the identity of Tom Craig and then present it to him during the interview. Sally, however, had decided against this. (I was later to find out she had other plans for stealing identities . . .)

The time in Rome was fantastic. My talk/presentation went as well as I could have hoped. It was incredible telling my little personal story to so many people from different countries. It felt like performing to the United Nations. The family and I were treated very well. We were put up in a luxurious hotel and taken to some incredible restaurants. Ours were the only children there so it was a real treat for them.

Although, because of schedules, I didn't have the opportunity to interview Tom Craig, I did manage to interview Fabio. And it was great fun. We played around with the whole interview style. For example, there was a shot of me asking him a question in English, then a shot of him answering in Italian, then a shot of me frowning and looking confused. (Even though I was filming on my own I managed to make it look as though there were two cameras filming at the same time – without ever once 'crossing the line'.) We then did it again with me asking the next question in Italian, him answering in English and me again looking confused. He played along really well. Eventually the questions were asked and answered, and his facts about fraud in Europe were genuinely fascinating. As with my Edinburgh show, I wanted the documentary to be interesting and factual as well as light-hearted.

Once I returned from Rome I continued my daily nine-to-five job of going into the production company offices. Having been self-employed for so many years it felt very strange following the routine of catching the same train, seeing the same people, going to the same place for lunch, catching the same train home, seeing the same people. I'm not sure how 'normal' people do it.

Every day in the office and every night at home I worked on the script. I also organised the interviews, planned all the stunts, met potential production crew (camera operators, editors, etc). On top of this, I had to deal with red tape over ANY ideas I put forward. Nothing could be approved until it had gone past a minimum of three people at the production company And then again at Channel 4.

The stunts I had planned were all to prove the ease of Identity Theft. I firstly intended to show the mistakes people made themselves, either by throwing away important documentation or by simply giving out their personal information. I then wanted to show how companies allowed Identity Theft to take place – as had happened to me – by not carrying out enough stringent checks. In addition to this I planned to speak to victims of fraud, share their stories and learn whether they themselves, or the companies with which they had dealt, were at fault.

To see the mistakes that people made themselves, I

decided that I would firstly pick a person at random and go bin-raiding – i.e. rummage through their bins in the early hours of the morning – to see if they had thrown away anything I could use to steal their identity.

I then planned on ringing another random person and pretending I was from their bank, to see if they would give me their personal details.

Finally I wanted to set up a little stall in a shopping centre and tell people that I could stop them from having their identity stolen – if they gave me all their personal information!

Before I started work setting up these stunts, I was called into a meeting with Sally the producer and Rebecca the executive at Channel 4 – the one to whom I had pitched the initial idea. They wanted to know how the programme was shaping up and what my plans were. I told them about the stunts and they seemed very pleased. However, they told me that the programme would also need something bigger – something that would attract attention and publicity. While I understood the reasoning for this – it was a television programme competing with many others in the same time slot – the idea of 'doing something bigger' had never been brought up before. I asked them what exactly they meant by 'bigger'. They told me that I would need to carry out something controversial, something that would get the programme noticed. I said that I would have a think. However, they told me that I needn't bother thinking, as they had already done that for me and they had decided that I would try to steal the identity of someone in authority.

I didn't like the sound of this. It all sounded a bit too

risky. When I had first mooted the idea of trying to steal the identity of Tom Craig – who had been the Head of Fraud at Scotland Yard when I'd had my identity stolen – they weren't keen on the idea. Now I knew why. They wanted me to go after someone in the public eye. They told me that I would have to try and fraudulently obtain documentation in the name of the then Prime Minister, Tony Blair.

I said no.

This wasn't the response they had expected. Or wanted.

Up until this point, all the meetings I'd had with them had been fun. We'd chatted about how much they were looking forward to seeing my stand-up show and how great the programme was going to be. Now, however, the mood had completely changed.

'Do you want to make this programme or not?!'

I was really taken aback.

'It's not too late for us to start working on one of the ideas we turned down.'

'Of course I want to make it,' I said. 'I'm just concerned about doing something . . . illegal.'

'We've spoken to the Channel 4 lawyers and they've told us that there should be no repercussions as it's in the public interest.'

When I had first agreed to make the programme, I had to sign a contract. The contract stated that in the 'unlikely' event of legal action being taken against me, Channel 4 would NOT provide me with legal assistance. I wouldn't sign it. They told me that there should be nothing to worry about as everything we were doing would be in the public interest and I had journalistic protection. I explained that if there genuinely was 'nothing to worry about' then surely they would have no problem in removing this clause and instead stating that in the 'unlikely' event of anything going wrong, they WOULD assign me legal assistance. This went back and forth between us until they reluctantly agreed to change the contract.

I was slowly starting to worry about it. Part of me thought about walking away from the whole thing. But if I did that then the past couple of months would have been a waste. And I really wanted to make the programme. So I gave it some thought. How bad could it really be? This was Channel 4. They constantly had investigative programmes and I had never heard of anyone being arrested for making one. Was I just worrying unnecessarily? After all, if I found myself in trouble, then so would they. And they had a huge legal team. And, realistically, it was very unlikely I'd get very far in my quest. I couldn't imagine easily obtaining any documentation for the Prime Minister!

So I agreed.

Not being a professional thief – I studied drama – I wasn't sure where to begin in my quest to steal Mr Blair's identity. I thought about the proof of ID used to open bank accounts, mobile-phone contracts, etc. This was usually a passport or driver's licence together with a utility bill or credit-card statement. However, to apply for a passport or driving licence you obviously needed proof of identity. It was a circle – albeit more 'irritating' than 'vicious'.

It was while looking into application forms for driving licences that I read about the plans for ID cards being proposed by the Home Secretary, Charles Clarke. Great, I thought, yet another way someone can fraudulently assume another person's identity. I was tempted to write to him and share my views on this idea, but I guessed that the thoughts of an unknown comedian wouldn't make him change his mind. And then it struck me. What if I proved to him how easy it was to obtain documentation of this type – by doing it to him? After all, if I did have to steal the identity of someone in authority then at least this gave me more of a reason. So I spoke with Sally and Rebecca and told them of my plan. Instead of trying to steal the identity of the Prime Minister, I would instead try to steal the identity of the Home Secretary. They loved the idea, especially as there now seemed an added justification for doing it.

Of course, even though I had changed the person, it didn't make the task any easier. This was still the Home Secretary. The security around him would surely be incredibly tight.

One of the proofs of identity that could be used to apply for a driving licence was a birth certificate. Charles Clarke's date of birth was in the public domain so I just needed to find his address. That took me almost three minutes. So I had his name, address and date of birth. That was all that was needed. The form for a birth certificate was filled in online and a postal order paid for by the production company.

The birth certificate was received in the office within a matter of days. But would that single proof of identity be enough to acquire a driving licence?

Within a few days I found out it was. A driving licence arrived with Charles Clarke's name and date of birth - and my photograph.

I couldn't believe it. None of us could. We had managed to obtain an important proof of identity in the name of the British Home Secretary. And it had been done so easily.

For legal reasons I can't explain exactly what was done to acquire it or how it was sent to a different address; after all, if you apply for a new driving licence, it should automatically be sent to the address on file. Suffice to say it was incredibly easy.

Once the licence had been received we immediately contacted the Home Office to set up a meeting. We explained about the documentary and told them that the meeting was to discuss Identity Fraud and ID cards. My plan was to film the meeting, with consent, and then hand over what I had managed to obtain. After all, the whole reason for doing this was to prove that there was a flaw in the system.

A meeting was set up for the following week with Andy Burnham, the then Parliamentary Under Secretary of State, who was working alongside Charles Clarke to implement ID cards.

While waiting for this meeting, I started my first proper day of filming – aside from the ones I had done myself in Rome – on 26 January 2006.

From my first day at the production company, I had been working alongside a young producer, Jessica, who was incredibly efficient and had experience in these types of programmes. Now she and I, together with Derek – the cameraman I had chosen from the ones I'd interviewed – drove to Nottingham to meet a victim of fraud.

I had researched the victim's story – someone had

bought a new, expensive car in her name – and planned how I wanted the interview to be shot. From the start, as stated in my pitch to Channel 4, I wanted this programme to address a serious topic yet still have an element of humour. So after interviewing the victim we then decided to see how easy it was to set up fake Facebook accounts and email addresses and contact friends of hers, offering various things, to see who would fall for them. This was fun and lightened the mood we'd set up with the interview earlier.

The following day I filmed my second interview. This was with Tom Craig. As he had been one of the speakers in Rome (even though I hadn't interviewed him there I had filmed a small part of his talk), I decided that I should interview him in an Italian restaurant to give the impression that we were in Rome. We would then come out to reveal it was in London – keeping the themes of fraud and deception that I wanted to run throughout the programme.

The interview was great. I told him what I had planned to do to him and he found it funny. He said he would have been interested to see how far I'd have managed to go. (I didn't tell him about the Home Secretary's driving licence in case it got back to the Home Office before my meeting with them.)

I asked him his opinion on ID cards and the general attitude of the police towards the crime of Identity Theft. His answers were very surprising. He was completely against ID cards. Like me he saw them as detrimental in stopping Identity Theft, as they were actually another method to carry out the crime. More importantly, he told me, on camera, how little regard the police have for Identity

Theft as a crime and for its victims. I was delighted with this interview and decided it would be part of the teaser trailer, which would go out before the programme.

I had interviews lined up for the following days and a huge list of things to organise. However I was already feeling exhausted. The truth was, since obtaining the driving licence, I'd hardly slept at all. I was so worried that I'd be arrested before I'd had the chance to explain everything to the Home Office. Every time there was a knock on the door I expected it to be the police, and every time I heard a police siren I assumed they were coming for me. I really wanted to make this programme, I just hoped that I hadn't made an awful mistake that I would later regret.

The next interview I had lined up was with Jim from Experian – one of the people who had really liked my Edinburgh show and had agreed to sponsor it. Again, although he gave me the facts and figures I needed, I wanted to try and lighten things up, so I added some visual comedy elements to the interview. Jim played along really well, but I was beginning to find it a little tricky both presenting and directing the programme, as I found myself being aware of how the shots looked instead of concentrating on what I was saying. I decided that, in future, I would storyboard things a little more so that the cameraman would know exactly what shots I wanted.

I was so pleased that I was being allowed to film this documentary in the way I had planned. Or so I thought. Little did I know that Sally, one of the producers, had no intention whatsoever of letting me have things my way and was just letting me carry on until she finished working on some other programmes.

The next interview – with my parents in Wales – was to give me the first indication that the production company had plans to make a completely different programme to the one I had intended . . .

Chapter 9

When Rosy and I had lost everything and had made the decision to live with my parents in Wales, it had been tough for everyone. However it was now years later and the stress and tension on both sides was long forgotten. So I was quite surprised when, while we were filming in Wales, Jessica – the young producer who was with me on the shoot – said that she wanted to take my parents individually to one side and interview them by herself on camera. This was something I had intended doing myself so I didn't quite understand why Jessica now wanted to do it or why she didn't want me there. I questioned her about it and she seemed quite evasive and uncomfortable. I explained that I wasn't prepared to continue shooting anything until I knew what was going on.

She eventually, reluctantly, told me that Sally had ordered her to get some 'emotional' shots. Sally had apparently told Jessica that she needed to get some friction between my parents and me, as it would make 'good television'. I was shocked. Look, I'm not naive, I know that things on television are manipulated, but I didn't expect someone to try to manipulate my own programme!

I immediately rang Sally and asked her what was going on. She was quite dismissive, simply explaining, before she hang up, that this was the way these types of programmes worked.

Well, not mine.

Although this documentary was about fraud and deception, I had no intention of misleading viewers. I wanted everything to be a true account of what had happened. I realised that Jessica was in a difficult position as she had received the demand from her superior. So I compromised. I told Jessica that she could interview my mother without my being there, and discuss what happened – but not to falsify anything or try and lead the conversation away from the subject matter. She agreed. (I also realised that I would be editing the programme, so if there was anything I didn't like, I could take it out.)

Apart from chatting with my parents in Wales – which was pretty emotional, as we were all remembering how difficult a time it had been – I carried out a stunt which I had been meticulously planning for the previous few weeks.

As I have mentioned, during the course of the programme I wanted to show how easy a crime Identity Theft is to carry out, not only because of the lack of checks carried out by companies but also because of the mistakes we make ourselves. So I decided to set up a little stall in a Swansea shopping centre where I would offer people free protection from Identity Theft – providing they gave me all their personal details. As I explained to them, unless they proved to me who they were, I couldn't protect them.

We arrived early at the shopping centre and my dad helped me set up. I'd had posters made with the wording: 'Identity Theft is the fastest growing crime in the UK –

protect yours here!' And: 'Is someone stealing your identity right now?' To make things more 'authentic', I wore a suit, made myself a badge and drew up some official-looking documentation for people to fill in.

The plan was that they would give me the account details and numbers of all the bank accounts/cards they wanted to protect. I really had no idea if the whole thing would work at all. There was every chance I would spend the day standing on my own, watching people walk past. However, from the moment I started setting up the stall, people were asking me about the service I was providing. By the time I began 'trading', there was already a long queue! It was incredible. People could not give me their private details quickly enough. I knew that ID fraud was in the news and that a high percentage of people in Wales were very concerned about it, but I had not expected such a big reaction to my little scam. They gave me their full names, addresses, dates of birth, passwords, card numbers, mother's maiden names, card verification code. . . everything I asked for.

Only one person questioned my authenticity.

One.

There was a great moment when a man gave me all his details, walked away, stopped, came back and said, 'Hang on – is this a scam?!' I looked at him, frowned and said, 'Of course not!'

'I just had to check,' he said, before happily walking off.

(I'm so pleased with this shopping centre scam that I still use the video clip as part of my Identity Theft talk around the world.)

So I had successfully proven that we as consumers are

one cause of ID theft by the way we easily give our private details to strangers face to face. But I wanted to find out if we also easily gave away information over the phone and if we literally threw away information that could be used to defraud us.

To discover this, I decided to choose two people at random. After returning to my parents' house following the shopping centre scam, I filmed myself looking through my comic-book collection in their attic. I liked the idea of linking the programme to comic books, not only because I'm a fan of them, but also because it was in keeping with the whole 'identity' theme.

While looking through the comic books it dawned on me that the random people I was going to choose should have the same name as a superhero. And I don't mean that I was going to look for a Mr Superman. I decided to find people called Peter Parker – the 'real' name of Spider-Man.

Once we had filmed this scene, Jessica told me that I would still have to run the idea past Sally before putting it into the programme. Of course I would. So when I returned to the office the following day I told Sally my plan. She didn't like it. Of course she didn't. She told me that no one would know who Peter Parker was. I explained that, apart from the popular comic books which had been in circulation since the Sixties, there had been Spider-Man films which had grossed over £100,000,000. She wasn't convinced. Of course she wasn't. So I offered her a deal: I would ask fifteen people in the office if they knew who Peter Parker was. If more than a third didn't, then I wouldn't do it. She agreed.

Out of the fifteen people, fourteen knew who he was.

The only person who didn't know was an older lady who thought that he might work in the accounts department.

So, now that it was agreed, I opened a central London telephone book and chose two people with the name Peter Parker. I obviously knew nothing about them, except for their name and the address printed in the book. By an incredible coincidence, they lived five minutes away from each other.

I had planned to use two methods of ID theft. Firstly I was going to ring one of the Mr Parkers, pretend I was calling from a bank and say that a new credit card had been applied for in his name and that I just needed to verify it was legitimate. The second method was much more hands-on. Literally. I would go to his house the night before bin-collection day, take his rubbish bags and see if he had thrown away anything of importance.

So, once I had worked on my script, I rang the first Peter Parker. As planned, I said I was from a bank and told him about the credit card. He was immediately worried – which is the reaction a good fraudster wants – and said that he knew nothing about it. I told him not to worry and that I would check everything. But before doing that I needed some details, including his date of birth, to verify that he was indeed Peter Parker. He gave me everything I asked for. I then ended the call by assuring him that the credit-card application would be stopped. He thanked me for my help.

It was that easy.

I had his name, address and date of birth – all within a matter of minutes. I decided that I would try and open a home shopping account in his name.

I knew that the second Peter Parker stunt would be a lot more difficult and might prove to be completely futile. I found what day the rubbish was collected at his house and planned with Jessica what I would do the night before.

We decided that I would drive to his house at 1 a.m. and, providing he had put his rubbish out, I would steal it! (NB When this programme was made we were all still using black bin bags as opposed to the wheelie-bin system that's now in place.)

I had spoken to a policeman friend of mine, who explained that taking someone's rubbish is classed as theft and could lead to a prison sentence. I brought this up with the Channel 4 lawyers, who told me that there 'should be' no problem as 'it is in the public interest'. Although I wasn't keen on 'should be', I accepted their guidance. After all, they were the lawyers.

The night of the Rubbish Raid was really, really stressful. Yet also, it has to be said, incredibly exciting. When we turned up at 1 a.m., there were police everywhere – but they were nothing to do with me! Although this Mr Parker lived in a lovely house, it wasn't in the nicest of locations.

There were a few coincidences with this house. Firstly, it was two minutes from a comedy club in which I played on a regular basis; secondly, the names of the streets all around were the same names as the streets I had grown up with in South Wales. It felt like a good omen (although had his house number been 666, I wouldn't have been so keen).

To fit the role and get into character, I had dressed all in black, with a black beanie hat and black gloves. In my head I was James Bond, although in truth I probably looked like the Black Magic Man who had eaten most of his own product. The gloves, which had been bought for me, were actually, by mistake, fishing gloves. This meant that they had slits in them for putting bait on hooks – not the most hygienic type for rummaging through rubbish.

Once we had set up the camera in the car – Derek the cameraman would sit in the passenger seat and film me first and then sit behind me and shoot in my rear-view mirror – we started filming.

I first drove past the house just to see if the rubbish bags were there. I know I could have checked this first, but I wanted to capture everything – delight, disappointment, frustration, etc. – on film.

Initially I couldn't see the bin bags and thought we would have to cancel the whole thing. Then I saw them, in a corner, outside his front door, behind his gate.

I parked the car outside the house and, leaving the engine running, got out and looked around. I then went to the gate, opened it as quietly as I could, took the bags, put them on the pavement in front of the gate, closed the gate, picked the bags up again, put them into the boot of my car and quickly drove off.

When I was eight years old I once stole a tiny badge from a shop. I hadn't intended on stealing it; I had been playing with it and then left the shop with my mother. That was the only crime I had ever committed. Until this moment. I'm fully aware this was hardly Ocean's Eleven, but it was still nerve-wracking and my heart was racing.

The next thing I had to do was film myself opening the bags to see if I was to be rewarded for my actions. The Channel 4 lawyers had explained that, for legal reasons, once I had rummaged through the rubbish, it all had to be put back in the bags and kept. Kept! We couldn't just throw it away! It all had to be returned at the end. This made no sense to me, but then I'm not paid for my legal expertise. So we went to Jessica's flat, put tarpaulin on the floor and emptied the bags.

If I didn't know better I would say that the whole thing had been set up. Incredibly, there, in amongst the egg-shells, used teabags and banana skins, were telephone bills, credit-card application forms and a PIN. He had torn the PIN in half and thrown it away. Both pieces were there. I could not have asked for a better result. I wasn't sure exactly what I could do with this information, or if it was enough, but felt like a great starting point.

I hardly slept for what was left of that night.

The following day we were due to film the opening shots of the programme. I had storyboarded this in exact detail. The idea was that we would follow some random person walking along the street while a voiceover would say, 'Bennett Arron is an award-winning writer and come-dian. He is also a major victim of Identity Theft . . .' Because of the way this style works, the viewer would assume that the person walking along was me. (The ad-vantage to not being famous is that no one knows what you look like!)

This shot would end as the person walked past me – leaving me speaking to the camera. I was very pleased with this idea and knew it would work well with the theme of the programme. (In truth it had actually been suggested by my friend Michael – the one who works in advertising – but I'd prefer not to give him the credit.)

As the person who stole my identity had been Nigerian, I wanted to use a Nigerian person for the opening shot. Apart from anything else, the fact they would look nothing like me would add to the idea. I am friendly with the comedian Stephen K. Amos, whose parents are from Nigeria, and had run the idea passed him. He loved it and agreed to be the 'person'. So we shot the scene. It took quite a few takes as the timing had to be perfect and we were filming in a busy high street where there were several wannabe TV stars who kept getting into shot. Eventually we finished the shoot and it looked great. We then also used Stephen for some shots in my house. I had taken photographs of him with Rosy and the kids and put them in a frame. I then filmed him in the kitchen, laughing and hugging Rosy while I stood outside looking through the window. I wanted to show that, although a fraudster doesn't literally take over your life, sometimes it feels as though they have.

While I was shooting with Stephen I received a call from the production company. The meeting with the Home Office had been cancelled . . .

I didn't know what to do. This meeting was to be the climax of the programme, the final scene, where I handed over the driving licence to prove how easy it had been to obtain. But now that the meeting was cancelled, not only did I not have an ending for the programme, but I was left holding the driving licence!

Speaking of the driving licence, I was meant to have filmed a scene which showed me putting it into the safe at the Channel 4 offices. However, the lawyers at Channel 4 had suddenly decided that Channel 4 shouldn't be seen getting involved in this, as they were worried about legal repercussions. Shouldn't get involved?! Legal repercussions?! Weren't they ones who told me I had to do it or they wouldn't let me make the programme?

As I didn't want to keep it in my house – and no one else wanted the responsibility – it was agreed that it would be kept in the safe of the production company. Unfortunately they didn't have a safe at their London office so it had to be done at their other office – in Scotland. So I went there and filmed it. As it so happens I was quite pleased with the way I filmed this, as I made it look as though it were CCTV footage.

But back to the cancelled meeting.

I was incredibly worried. My only option was to try and reschedule it. I rang several times to try and speak with someone at the Home Office. I was told that someone would get back to me. All I could do was wait.

This must have been playing on my mind quite a bit as it affected one of the scams I was attempting to pull off – at least that's my excuse for messing it up.

I had attempted to open an account with a home shopping company under the name of the first Peter Parker, the one who had given me his date of birth over the phone. I thought it was all going well, until I received a letter from their customer services department informing me that they needed further proof of identity and needed 'Peter Parker' to call them. So, after setting up the camera to film it, and with his address and date of birth to hand, I rang customer services. They told me that they needed to confirm 'my' details with me. They asked for my address, which I gave, and my date of birth, which I also happily gave. They then asked me how old I was. I wasn't expecting this. I quickly attempted to work out his age. It was a simple maths sum. And I got it wrong! I was ten years out! They told me that I had failed the security questions and that the account would not be opened. I should have been pleased that they had such stringent measures in place. But I was too annoyed over the fact that I'd messed up. All the trouble I had gone to, to obtain his date of birth, had been for nothing.

I had to put all this behind me and work on the next part of the project – to film the show I had performed at the Edinburgh festival. I had chosen a venue near Great Portland Street. It was a small basement theatre where I had performed in several sketch shows. The plan was to film it twice in one day – once late afternoon and then again in the evening – with two different audiences. Because I would be wearing the same clothes, we would be able to combine shots of myself and the audience from both shows. I was quite nervous about doing it. Even though I had performed it for three weeks in Edinburgh and then in Rome, that had been more than three months ago. And, in addition, this time it was being filmed for TV. I found that as I was performing the shows, I was thinking of where each bit would drop into the programme and how it would link the whole thing together.

I needn't have worried. Rosy came to both shows and she told me how well they went. As a performer you are sometimes unaware when things go well – although you definitely know when they go really badly. Sally also attended the shows. I can only assume that the reason she didn't laugh at all was because she was concentrating on the production aspect . . .

After the shows, Rosy and I went out for dinner. (I should have claimed back the cost of the babysitter from Channel 4!) Although I still had the worry of the cancelled Home Office meeting hanging over me I was in a good mood. The programme was generally falling into place. I'd interviewed a few potential editors and chosen the one who seemed to understand the look and feel I was after.

The following day I gave this chosen editor the stand-up footage and together we started to work together on the edit. This was the part of the process to which I'd been really looking forward. I love the concept of editing, and in my mind I already knew the general shape of the programme.

The editor and I first worked on the scenes in Rome, then the meeting with Jim from Experian, then the opening title sequence with Stephen K. Amos. It took all day and early evening but by the end, although it was just a rough cut, it all looked good. It was the mix of funny and serious I had wanted.

Because I had been working flat out both day and night, Sally had actually allowed me a day off. So, the following day, having left the editor with my notes about editing the stand-up material, I went to Elstree Studios to watch one of my episodes of the children's programme Genie in the House being filmed. It looked great, although it was odd just watching and not being able to direct it!

When I returned to the office the following day I discovered exactly why I had been given the day off. While I had been at Elstree Studios, Sally had gone into the editing suite and completely changed the edit. The scenes in Rome had been cut, the interview with Jim from Experian had been cut, everything that was remotely funny or amusing had also been cut – including all my stand-up! Sally had decided that there was no place for a 'comedy routine' in the documentary.

I was devastated.

The programme I had pitched, the programme I had wanted to make, was about to be replaced by a dull, serious, documentary-by-numbers.

I wanted to cry.

Chapter 10

Ironically, the last time I had been this stressed and upset was when my identity had been stolen. Sally had sent me a text message suggesting that I needn't bother coming back to work with the editor again as she was now taking over that side of things.

I had put so much into this programme – planning, storyboarding, working on stunts, writing the script until 2 o'clock in the morning, being away from the family – yet it didn't seem to matter. A part of me now wanted to walk away from the whole thing. I no longer cared if the programme was ever aired or not.

But I knew I couldn't just walk off. I still had this bloody driving licence and I needed to try to rearrange the meeting with the Home Office. I had no option but to stay.

I also had one piece of bargaining power . . .

I sent Sally a five-page text message. I told her that, as my name was attached to the programme – and my family were in it – they couldn't air it without my consent and that unless I had the creative input into the production which I'd been promised, then that consent would not be given.

She replied by 'inviting' me into the office the following morning for a chat. She told me to work on a new draft of the script and bring it with me. I worked on that script until 3a.m. and went in for the meeting at ten. Sally looked at the script, and then, literally, put it in the bin. We then started our chat. You can imagine the atmosphere.

As if things weren't bad enough, during our lovely conversation I received a call from the South Wales Police. Someone from the shopping centre in Swansea had made a complaint against me. Apparently their bank account had been hacked and they thought I was to blame! I explained that all the details I had taken had been immediately shredded – and that I had filmed myself doing it. The police said that they would still have to investigate. Great.

Sally and I attempted to find a compromise over the editing. There were still several scenes to be shot, but there was no way I was filming them if they were then just going to be taken away from me and ruined in the edit.

A new person had also joined the team: Hilary, an experienced documentary producer. I hoped, prayed, that Hilary would understand what I wanted to do.

Rebecca, the executive at Channel 4, had asked to see a rough edit of the first half of the programme. So Sally, Hilary and I went to her office to show it to her. She watched it and then asked why there were 'funny' bits in it – even though, as she explained, she didn't actually find them funny herself.

I reminded her that, when I had pitched the programme, I said it would be a mixture of seriousness and humour. She told Sally and Hilary that she didn't want that any more. They agreed. She then told them what had to be changed. They agreed. Why wouldn't they? This was just another programme to them and they wanted to make more of them. The fact that it was my own personal story was irrelevant. As you can tell, my attendance at that meeting had been pointless.

When we all returned to the office Hilary and Sally had a private meeting. They emerged from this to tell me that they were cutting some more scenes. They were taking out Tom Craig's views on the police as they were too controversial (he had been a Scotland Yard officer – his views were important!) and they were cutting all the scenes with Stephen K. Amos as they were worried that it would be deemed racist. I tried to explain, once again, that Stephen looked similar to the person who stole my identity – and the fact he looked NOTHING like me helped to make the point. Stephen had been happy to play the role as it was just like a part in a film or play. (I imagined them having to produce a production of Othello and deciding that the actor should be white so as not to offend anyone!)

While this debate went on, we suddenly received a call from the Home Office. The meeting was back on and it was happening in two days' time!

I had to forget about everything else and concentrate on this meeting.

I knew exactly what I was going to do and say. I was going to show all the facts and figures about Identity Theft and explain why it wasn't a 'victimless crime'. I would then give my views on Identity Cards and explain why companies should stop sending out pre-printed application forms. (As far as I'm concerned, if you can't write your own name and address on an application for a credit card, you shouldn't be allowed to have one.) To prove all these points, I would then, dramatically, produce Charles Clarke's driving licence and hand it over. If it all went as I envisaged, it would be a great ending for the programme.

For the first time in weeks I was actually quite excited. We booked a camera crew and cancelled the other filming arrangements we'd made for that day.

The next day the Home Office cancelled again. And we were told, categorically, that they were too busy to re-schedule.

They knew! There was no other explanation. They must have found out what I had done and knew that I was going to present the driving licence. But how? And if that were the case, was I now going about to be arrested? I started to panic. I knew I had to do something. I told Hilary and Sally that I wanted to doorstep Charles Clarke and hand him the licence. I explained that I could either do it as he left the House of Commons or, as I had his home address, I could do it there. Sally thought it wasn't a bad idea at all. But Hilary didn't agree. I asked her why and she said she was worried about his bodyguard. I didn't even know Charles Clarke had one. Hilary told me that the bodyguard would act instinctively and think of consequences later. I was surprised she knew so much. But what options did that leave? Hilary suggested that I just wrote a nice letter to Charles Clarke, telling him what I had done, and giving him the right to reply. But how dull an ending to the pro-gramme would that be? All that work just to put a letter on the screen – providing he would even reply.

I was now getting desperate. Everything was falling apart.

At home that night I was very down. I had been difficult to live with throughout this whole experience as the pressure and lack of sleep had made me tense and irritable. I was snapping at everything and everyone. I had never regretted anything in my life and had never wanted to. However, I was now beginning to regret ever getting involved in this programme.

On the way into the office the following day I suddenly had an idea. What if I stood outside the Houses of Parliament – on the day of Prime Minister's Questions – holding a huge placard with a copy of the driving licence. Charles Clarke would see it as he was either arriving or leaving. I suggested it to both Hilary and Sally and, incredibly, they both agreed to the idea.

However, when I looked into the practicalities, I discovered that a very recent law had banned protesters from being within half a mile of Parliament Square. So I couldn't do that. Then I wondered about the possibility of finding out the route Charles Clarke would take to go to Westminster. If I knew it, I could stand somewhere prominent on the route, outside the half-mile exclusion zone, holding my placard. It was a thought. Hilary then, bizarrely, told me that she would probably be able to find out the route! I was surprised but delighted.

While I was organising the printing of the placard, South Wales Police rang back to say that there was no evidence linking me to the fraudulent bank account. Small mercies.

Also that day I received an order of shoes from a catalogue company. I had managed to open an account in the name of the bin-raided Peter Parker and, in keeping with the whole Spider-Man theme, had ordered four pairs of identical shoes (a spider has eight . . . oh, you get the idea).

Jessica, the young producer who had been working alongside me, contacted Peter Parker, explained briefly what I was doing and asked if he would be happy to meet me. Fortunately he said yes. So a meeting was arranged at his house where I would be filmed handing over everything I had taken from his bins and showing him what I had managed to do with his discarded information.

So I had three scenes left to film: the one with Peter Parker, the scene near Parliament and a scene – which Sally had insisted upon – of me standing outside the house I had wanted to buy and angrily throwing stones into a pond. This scene sounded ridiculous and, unlike the rest of the programme, really false and contrived. But I was too tired to argue any more. I just wanted to get the whole thing finished and try to get back to some semblance of a normal life.

The filming with Peter Parker went better than I could have hoped. I had dressed up as Peter Parker from the Spider-Man comics – complete with glasses and camera – and knocked on Mr Parker's house. When he opened the door, I was more shocked than him. He looked almost identical to the way I had dressed! I had had no idea what he would be like so this was a really funny bonus. I just hoped that, because it was funny, it wouldn't be cut out.

I showed him what I had taken from his bins and he was shocked. He couldn't believe he had thrown away so many documents with so much detail on them. I explained to him that, had I been a professional criminal, I would have been able to contact his bank and change his address. Then when 'he' received a new credit/debit card – at the new address – I could have used them.

I also told him that I could even have taken money from his account. He asked me how I could do that without his PIN. I showed him the number he had ripped in half and thrown away. His reaction was fantastic. I could not have scripted it better.

I left his house, discarded my Peter Parker costume – with a lovely in-reference for comic-book fans – and prepared for the next big, important scene . . .

Hilary had given me the route that Charles Clarke would take from Norwich to the Houses of Parliament (I still didn't know how she knew) and I had marked out my territory from Parliament Square. The closest intersection would be on Waterloo Bridge, one of my favourite bridges in London.

I had two placards, one with an enlarged picture of Charles Clarke's driving licence and the other with the words 'Mr Clarke – Your Identity is in My Hands'.

I stood on the bridge, in the wind and rain, holding the signs up to all passing vehicles. I stood there for two hours – until I knew that Prime Minister's Questions had started.

He didn't pass by.

That was it. I was done. Sally said that I would now have to write to Scotland Yard and the DVLA, telling them what I had done and why I had done it. Sally wrote the letter on the production company's letterhead paper and I signed it for her to send. I would now have to film myself cutting up the driving licence. It wasn't anything like the ending I had planned, but I just needed the awful experience to finish. I wanted to get back to spending evenings at home with my family.

I knew there were some more scenes to film, including

the ending, and that there would be more arguments over the editing, but I was at least beginning to see the end . . .

The rest of the filming went according to plan. I agreed to the ridiculous 'throwing stones into a pond' shot and filmed the ending.

All that was left was the voice-over. Sally and Hilary had decided that I should do this myself – after all it was my story and my journey. I agreed. It was almost the first time we had agreed on anything. However, the agreements stopped when they presented me with the 'script' I would be saying. It was awful. It was clichéd and dull and, more importantly, didn't sound like me at all. There was no element of fun or excitement. I said I wouldn't do it. They told me that I HAD to do it. I tried to calmly explain that they would have difficulty, except under torture, of making me say words I didn't want to say. I told them that I would rewrite it. They told me that as it was being recorded the following day I only had that night to do it. If I couldn't get it done, then we would record their script.

That night, after arriving home from the office at nine thirty, I stayed up until 4 a.m. rewriting what they had written. After hearing the phrase 'Why is this funny?' more than fifty times since I had started working on the programme, I knew better than to try and put in anything too amusing . . .

The next morning at seven thirty I was sitting in the editing suite on my own watching the film to time it for the voice-over I had written. As I watched it, tears were streaming down my face. It could have been because I was tired, it could have been because it was almost over or it could have been because the past nine months had left me physically and emotionally drained. Whichever it was, I knew that I would never experience anything like this ever again. And I was delighted about that. I'd learned a lot, mainly about a type of person in this industry. This type of person looks, talks and dresses in a certain way. They're not willing to take creative risks, but when something does accidentally sneak through and does well, they are willing to take the credit.

People who are unable to construct a coherent sentence are telling writers how to write, people who have no creative vision are telling directors how to direct, and people who have no sense of humour are telling comedians what's funny. I also learned that, in future, I needed to have as much creative control as possible over my work. Which made me appreciate performing stand-up so much more.

My new script, with a few alterations, was agreed and we recorded the voice-over. I have to say Sally was very complimentary of my voice-over ability. It was virtually all done in one take. Once it was completed it had to be delivered to the Channel 4 lawyers and Rebecca in case they wanted to make any last-minute changes.

I had expected the odd change or query here and there but what I hadn't expected was a long document back from the lawyer, completely taking the programme apart and querying some very odd things. For example, she wanted to know why, when stealing the bin bags, did I say, 'I could be going down for a ten stretch'? Did I know for a fact whether this was the correct jail sentence for committing such a crime? Trying to explain to her that it was 'just a joke' was futile.

While I was more concerned about that I was seen to be

signing the driving licence application, she wanted to know why I had referred to climbing the ladder into my parents' attic as 'getting on the property ladder'.

(By the way, I REALLY hadn't wanted to film the signing of the driving licence form but Sally, who was with me on the day of that part of the shoot, had insisted, saying that it HAD to be seen on film. I'd reluctantly agreed, not realising this action would be my biggest mistake).

I argued my case as much as I could, but I was so drained from battling against everyone, I conceded to many of their requests.

A few days later, after the changes had been made, the programme was done.

Finished.

I couldn't remember being so relieved about anything. Although I had hated almost every moment of making it, at least now it was over. And I was proud of what I had achieved. It would have just been better without going into the depressing office, arguing over things I wouldn't do or say and trying to explain to people with no sense of humour why something was funny.

I could get back to my life and wait for the programme to eventually be aired on TV.

And then Charles Clarke was fired.

Chapter 11

On 5 May 2006, because of a scandal involving the deportation of foreign prisoners, Charles Clarke was fired as Home Secretary.

The minute this came on the news I contacted Sally and asked if there was any way the programme could be shown sooner rather than later. She came back to me and said that she had spoken to Rebecca about it but Rebecca wasn't interested. Apparently Rebecca had said that she was no longer a fan of the programme. Nice. However, even without Rebecca's interest, it still apparently had to be shown as part of Channel 4's New Directors Scheme.

I suggested to Sally that I redo the voice-over at the end, mentioning Charles Clarke's departure and stating how I hoped the new Home Secretary would give Identity Theft the attention it needed. She agreed.

The thought of going back into the office made me feel sick. But I had to. So I recorded the new voice-over piece and left as quickly as I could.

As I left I bumped into one of the other directors I'd met at the pitch meeting and who was also just finishing his programme. He told me how he had hated the experience and how almost everything he had wanted to put into the programme had been refused.

I had loved the programme idea he had pitched, but from the sound of it, it was no longer that film but instead now another documentary-by-the-book. We shared empathy.

That night, Rosy, the kids and I went to the premiere of *Genie in the House* in a cinema in the West End. It was great fun and helped me to forget about the programme for a while.

But not for long.

I received a call early the following morning and was told that the lawyer wanted me to send her a detailed signed letter of all the 'illegal' acts I'd committed. Surely she meant: 'asked to commit if I wanted the programme to be made',

So I did. There was little point in not doing it, as it was all there on film.

Speaking of letters, I was surprised that there had been no response to the letters Sally had sent to the DVLA and Scotland Yard. Maybe they completely understood what I had done and saw no problem with it. Maybe they agreed this would be a good way of showing the loopholes so that it didn't genuinely happen to someone.

A wrap party had been booked, where clips from all the documentaries would be screened. Our neighbour babysat for the children so Rosy and I could go along. We watched the other films. They looked pretty good – although I could tell by the faces of most of the other directors that they weren't what they had wanted. Then mine was shown. It looked good. Unfortunately all anyone could do was look – as they had forgotten to add the sound! Rosy was really upset. As far as I was concerned, this perfectly summed up the whole experience.

Although I had been able to perform at a few gigs throughout the shoot, I hadn't worked as much as usual so things were financially a bit tight. However, Genie in the House was doing well on Nickelodeon and it looked as if it would be going to a second series, which was great news. I had meetings lined up with various producers about scripts and game-show ideas. I also had magazine articles to write and I was working on a book (not this one – not yet). It was going to take me a while to get back into a normal routine, but I was looking forward to it.

I occasionally received round-robin emails from the production company giving everyone updates on the transmission dates for the programmes. Even though all the other programmes had theirs, there still wasn't a date for mine. I didn't know why.

There had still not been any reply to the letter Sally had sent to the various authorities, informing them what I had done. Surprisingly I was the only one who seemed concerned about this.

Eventually I received an email with the subject line 'Transmission Date'. I was very excited. Until I read the email. My programme was being shown on Thursday 7 September 2006. At 1 o'clock in the morning!!

The others were being shown at 9 or 10 p.m. But not mine.

All that time, energy and trauma for a programme no one would see. There was also a note from the PR department asking me if I would be happy to do press and publicity for the programme! What was the point? There'd be so few people watching it, I might as well go to their houses and tell them about it individually.

I rang Sally. She was also disappointed with the time slot it had been given but told me it had been a decision between Rebecca and the person who organises the scheduling. All the other documentaries had been on at a good time in the evening. Why had mine been pushed to what is known in TV as the 'graveyard slot'? Was it THAT bad?

So the programme was going to be shown in four months' time in the middle of the night. It was awful. But not as awful as when, two weeks prior to this transmission date, I was arrested . . .

Part Three

_____

Operation Hydrogen

Chapter 12

I know it sounds ridiculous, but I had more or less forgotten about what I had done. It was now almost a year since I had actually committed the 'crime' and, as there had been no repercussions, I assumed there would be no problems. Which explains why I didn't associate it with the loud banging on my front door at 6.50 one morning.

The previous night Rosy and I been out to celebrate our tenth wedding anniversary. It had been a late night – as our babysitter pointed out numerous times – and we were hoping to sleep in a bit, or at least for another half an hour until the alarm was due to sound. So, muttering some sleepy alliteration along the lines of 'probably . . . postman . . . parcel', I had clambered out of bed and gone downstairs. There, through my sleep-encrusted eyes and the frosted glass of the front door, I could make out three shapes. I thought that if it were a parcel it must be a HUGE one!

I opened the door to discover two men and a woman. They were dressed in suits and holding folders. My first thought was that they were either very keen Jehovah's Witnesses or timeshare salespeople. Either way, I wouldn't really be interested in what they were selling.

'Are you Bennett Arron?'

I nodded and hoped the next question would be just as easy.

They then showed me their identification and introduced themselves. They were from CID.

'You obviously know why we're here.'

As I mentioned earlier, I had genuinely forgotten what I had done. The fact that no one at Channel 4 seemed interested in the programme, and that hardly any viewers would be watching it in the earlier hours of the morning, meant I had put the whole thing to the back of my mind. So I stood there trying to figure out what was going on.

I knew that a few months earlier I had been flashed by a speed camera yet had not been issued with a ticket. Surely that wasn't it. I tried to think what else it could be; I was a month behind on my Council Tax, but they usually sent a reminder first.

'No,' I said. 'I don't.'

They seemed genuinely surprised. They were probably wondering how many crimes I had actually committed.

'You are suspected of applying for a driving licence in the name of the Home Secretary.'

I felt sick. I could hear my heartbeat banging in my ears.

'But . . . but . . . Channel 4 told me it would be in the public interest.'

They looked at me. 'Well . . . it's not!'

And that was that. My defence had been quashed in three words. It would have been four but they had used the apostrophe.

'Can we come in?'

I was surprised by my own lack of courtesy. I stepped

back and allowed the three of them to enter. I directed them to the living room and followed them in.

They looked around the room and then turned to me.

'Now, Mr Arron, we know you have children . . .'

I was amazed by the information they had on me. And no doubt the pictures of the children around the room had helped.

'. . . so we don't want to have to search your house and disturb them. However, we will be forced to do that unless you supply us with all your paperwork for the programme, including copies of application forms, emails, letters, etc.'

I told them that I had everything upstairs in the bedroom and that I would go and retrieve it. In retrospect I believe I should have asked them if they had a search warrant. At the time I didn't think of it. I suppose I'm not that au fait with criminal etiquette.

As I was about to leave the room, the female officer added, 'Oh, and you might like to get dressed as well.'

It was only then I realised that I had been standing there all this time wearing just my Bugs Bunny pyjama bottoms.

I went upstairs to the bedroom. Rosy was sitting up in bed. She'd heard what was going on.

'What are they going to do?'

'I'm not sure.'

I then went through all my files and folders.

'Are you going to call anyone?'

'I don't know.'

Yasmin came into the room. She wanted to know who had been banging on the door. She was hoping it was one of the regular parcels sent by Rosy's mum from Spain, which are always crammed with a selection of toys, photographs, clothes and sweets. It was like our own free home shopping company – but one that was more careful about the addressee.

I told her that some people had come to talk to me about the documentary. As she'd seen a succession of producers, camera operators, etc. coming to the house, she happily accepted this explanation. I gathered all the information together, changed from my jimjams and went back downstairs. One of the officers, the Detective Sergeant (who I shall refer to as DS) was looking at a writing award placed surreptitiously on the mantelpiece.

'So you're a writer as well as a comedian.'

I didn't know if this was a question or statement (which is why I haven't put a question mark at the end) but either way this was the type of conversation I'd hoped to have on a TV chat show, not in my living room with a CID officer at 7 o'clock in the morning. I nodded and handed over the paperwork to the male Detective Constable (DC-M) together with a DVD copy of the documentary.

'Is this everything?' he asked.

'As far as I know,' I replied.

He handed it to the female Detective Constable (DC-F) and asked her to label it all.

He then turned back to me: 'Bennett Arron, I am arresting you on suspicion of falsely applying for and acquiring a driving licence in the name of Charles Clarke. You do not have to say anything, but it may harm your defence if you do not mention when questioned something which you later rely on in court. Anything you do say may be given in evidence.'

It was like a bad dream, as though I'd eaten a cheese

and onion sandwich while watching an old episode of *The Bill* and then gone straight to bed.

Then, in keeping with all the clichés I'd ever heard from television police shows, they told me that I had to accompany them to the station. They suggested I only took my bare essentials, as I'd have to hand in all my belongings and it would just take up time if I had too many things. I asked them if I could go and tell my wife. They weren't sure about this and looked at each other for advice. I didn't know what they expected me to do – jump out of the bathroom window and do, what I believe, is called a 'runner'?

Eventually they agreed, on the proviso that she wouldn't call anyone at the production company or Channel 4, as they didn't want to warn them. Warn them about what??

I went upstairs and, trying to hide my nervousness, quietly told Rosy that they were taking me in for questioning and that she mustn't call anyone associated with the programme. I told her that I would probably only be there an hour or so and would call her as soon as I could. I kissed her, kissed Yasmin and then went to kiss Xander, who was still fast asleep in his room. As I watched him sleeping I started to question what I had done.

I had simply set out to prove a point. I wanted to show how easy it was to steal someone's identity and potentially ruin their lives. And I had done that. I had stolen the identity of the Home Secretary – and I had done it very easily. Yet was it my place to do it? What consequences would this now have on me? What consequences would it have on my wife and children? Was it fair on them?

'Mr Arron?'

The voice from downstairs, so alien in my home, brought me back. I went down to find the three of them standing at my front door.

'Let's go.'

As we walked to the car I looked around, hoping that none of the neighbours were watching.

'You're lucky we decided not to cuff you,' said DC-F, obviously aware of my discomfort.

'Or use this,' she added, opening the boot of the car and showing me a large battering ram.

A battering ram?! I have a bell!

As DC-M opened the car door for me, the thought struck me for the first time: Why were there three of them? What had they been expecting? I'm five foot seven and a half, and overweight. The female officer could have taken me on her own.

As we started our journey a call came through on their radio. Apparently the station to which they had intended to take me was full. They now had to call around to find another station. A station that had a free cell.

A cell!

I was really being arrested!

Eventually they were told that there was a space at Harrow Road Police Station, almost twenty miles away.

We drove off.

After about ten minutes of silence, DS spoke.

'So . . . do you know Ricky Gervais?'

Not the type of hard-hitting interrogation question I was expecting.

'Er . . . yes.'

'I like him,' continued DS. 'He's very funny. Got some good lines.'

'I like Jim Davidson,' said DC-M.

There followed a discussion between the two of them as to which comedians were good and which weren't. I would normally have joined in, but I just wasn't in the mood.

'So,' said DC-F, 'you play a lot of the comedy clubs then?'

I felt that I was being interviewed by a tabloid journalist, as though every question was a trick to try to get information out of me.

'Yes,' I replied, throwing caution to the wind.

'You'll probably be writing about us in one of your routines!'

'No, I won't,' I lied.

The rest of the journey was taken up by them asking me what famous people I knew and telling me how no one had respect for the police any more.

'We constantly get abused by the public' said DC-M.

'But I bet you're their first point of call when they're in trouble,' I offered.

They all nodded in unison.

I felt we'd bonded. For a moment I forgot my situation and started enjoying the conversation. However, the sight of the police sign outside Harrow Road station quickly reminded me.

I was taken in through the rear of the station. We then all had to wait while a 'disturbance' was being seen to inside. Apparently a drunken man from the night before, who was yet to sober up, fancied having a fight with someone. I didn't see what happened, but from the noises it sounded as if someone had obliged – and he'd lost. Eventually we were allowed in. My arresting officers introduced themselves to the Desk Sergeant. That's when I found out that they had travelled from Scotland Yard to arrest me and not just from a local station. I was obviously more important than I had suspected. Even though I was visibly shaking, a part of me was hoping they'd start referring to me as 'Mr Big'.

An arrest report was written out and I was given a custody number. The report stated that my manner was 'Quite Calm'. I guess they weren't allowed to write 'crapping himself'.

As warned, I had to hand over all my possessions and sign for them. Even though I had taken the bare minimum in my trouser pockets, I had forgotten to check in my jacket. These are the items they wrote down on my property sheet:

Four pens
One mobile phone
Eleven keys on ring
One phone charger
One notebook
One diary

I know what you're thinking – eleven keys! In truth, six of these were tiny ones for suitcase locks – and three of those locks are actually broken so I have no idea why I still kept them.

After handing over all my belongings I was taken to a room where I had my photo taken. Then they put a swab in my mouth and took a DNA sample. This wasn't physically painful, but psychologically it really left a scar.

It was at this point I discovered that my case had been given a code name. I was 'Operation Hydrogen'. Even in my stressed and upset state I was quietly proud of this. I also thought it would be a good title for a James Bond film.

I was asked if I wanted to contact a lawyer. I told them that I wanted to speak with the Channel 4 lawyer as she was the one who knew about the case. This request was denied. Apparently there was a relatively new law which stated that if the requested lawyer is close to the case, that lawyer shouldn't be informed of an arrest in case they destroy any evidence.

They told me that officers were on their way to the production company and that once they were satisfied that they had all the evidence they required, I would then be allowed to speak with the Channel 4 lawyers.

I was allowed one phone call. I had always thought this was made up, but it's genuine. One phone call. I contemplated asking them if they had Charles Clarke's number. Instead I asked if I could call my wife. They told me that I could, but the call would be monitored and I could not ask her to contact the production company or Channel 4.

So I rang Rosy and told her what was happening. I told her not to worry and that I would hopefully be back soon. I asked her to kiss the kids for me. I know that sounds slightly melodramatic, but I didn't know whether I was about to go straight to jail.

After the call, I was taken to my cell.

Once they had locked the door, the viewing hatch was opened and I was asked if I wanted anything to eat or drink. I said that I wasn't really hungry. Being arrested somehow ruins your appetite. However it was suggested that I eat something as I would probably be there for a long time. That didn't really help.

'Why don't you just have some tea and toast?'

'Okay. Thanks.'

'Do you want sugar in the tea?'

'I don't normally, but today I will. Two spoons, please.'

'Okay.'

'Oh, and could I possibly have a pen and some paper as well, please?'

'Er . . . I'll see what I can do.'

The hatch closed.

I looked around my cell. I will never complain about a budget hotel room again. The cell was empty, save for a bed which was actually an extension of the concrete floor, with what looked like a school gym mat on top. The only other thing in the room was a small metal toilet. I was hoping that even though I was scared I wouldn't have to use it much.

The cell was around six feet wide by eight feet long. I measured it. Quite a few times.

The hatch opened again.

'Here you go.'

The officer passed me a pen and some paper. They'd obviously discussed it and decided that I wouldn't be using them as weapons. Little did they know the power of the paper cut.

I didn't know how long I was going to be in this cell, but what I did know was that I had to keep myself occupied. I write a regular column for the Welsh Men's magazine *Red Handed* and, as the deadline was approaching, I had planned to write my piece that day. In my living room. However, I decided that I would now write it in my cell instead.

I've never written an article so quickly. It's funny how having no distractions, like telephone/email/social-networking sites/school pick-up, can help you concentrate so much better. I thought about asking if I could use the cell as an office occasionally.

After finishing the article, I stared at the walls for a while and then drew some three-dimensional squares – I'm sure there's some deep psychological reason. I then actually started writing this book. I know how odd that must sound, but I had to do something. As I couldn't speak to anyone, and as I have written every day since I was in my early twenties – be it part of a book, play, sitcom script, etc. – this seemed the best way of dealing with the situation.

I initially started with this:

I am sitting in a cell in Harrow Police Station. This has put me off doing anything illegal ever again. In fact, if I am ever given too much change in a supermarket, I will not only give back the extra amount but I will also insist they sign a form in triplicate stating that I have done so.

Then I crossed it out, drew some more squares and wrote some of what you have already read. I then followed on with this . . .

Ironically one of my biggest fears is being sent to jail. It was always the bit I dreaded most when playing Monopoly.

So I'm sitting in a cell at Harrow Road Police Station not knowing what the hell is going to happen. Initially I was hoping I wouldn't be here more than an hour, but that was now over six hours ago.

My writing was interrupted by the door opening and the custody sergeant asking me to accompany him to the interrogation room.

When I was eventually returned to my cell I immediately wrote the following. Reading over it now, I can't believe that this is what I actually wrote in the cell. Although I was obviously incredibly anxious it seems so flippant at times. I suppose this is the way I have always dealt with emotional situations . . .

16.22. My hand is actually shaking as I am writing this. I have just been returned to my cell after being interviewed. I was taken from the cell over an hour ago. As I was walked past the front desk I noticed my name on the large Arrest/Detention Board.

CELL 8: ARRON   CHARGE: FRAUD

I have never been so scared. I was taken into a cell to be interviewed by the two male arresting officers. I don't know where the female was and it seemed odd to ask.

They sat me down and switched on an old-fashioned tape recorder to record the interview. One of them then said to me;

'Right Mr Arron, we've watched your documentary . . .'

I don't know why, probably because I was nervous, but I genuinely said; 'Do you think I looked fat in it?'

Honestly. It will be on the recording.

He then said; 'No, I thought you looked all right. I really enjoyed it.'

Then the other officer said; 'Well I didn't enjoy it, I thought it was rubbish. Who's going to want to watch that?'

I thought, well, they're obviously playing 'Good Reviewer, Bad Reviewer'.

They then asked me a series of questions. I asked again if I were allowed to speak with the lawyer at Channel 4. My request was denied. They told me that they had just received a search warrant for the production company offices and didn't want me calling them to 'tip them off' in case they destroyed any evidence!

So I answered all their questions completely honestly. I told them that, yes, I had applied for a birth certificate in the name of the Home Secretary; it was on the programme they had just watched. Yes, I had applied for and received the driving licence; there was a copy of it in the files I had given them. So everything I was asked I answered truthfully. I felt I had nothing to hide. Halfway through I felt sick and dizzy and asked if the interview could be stopped for a break. They agreed and I was given some water. When I was ready to speak again they told me that they wanted to speak with my accomplice. I didn't know what they were talking about. I asked them if they meant my producer or the cameraman. They said no, they didn't want to speak with either of them, they wanted to speak to my accomplice Daniel Skies. I told them that I had no idea who that was. They didn't believe me. They told me that holding back information or trying to protect someone would cause me more problems. I honestly didn't know what they were talking about or who Daniel Skies was. They then showed me some documentation with the name Daniel Skies on it. It *suddenly made sense. I explained that Daniel Skies was a name I made up so as not to use my real name. They didn't believe me. I then pointed to the signature on the forms I had 'signed'. The signature read 'D. Skies'. When they eventually got it, they had to get up and go to the back of the room to laugh so that it wasn't picked up on the recording!*

Eventually, after two hours, the interview ended. I have now been brought back into the cell. They just told me as they locked the door that there's every chance this case is going to the High Court and that I'll be going to jail. I feel as if I'm going to pass out.

I stopped writing. I was eventually released from the police station after twelve hours, distraught and shaking. I'd been released on police bail and told that I would have to return on 3 October.

I rang my brother, who was shocked to hear what had happened. He picked me up from a pub near the station and took me home. I could hardly speak on the journey – and not because of the large whisky I had drunk. When I arrived home I went upstairs and cried. I couldn't believe what had just happened. I fully understood that what I had done was, in the eyes of the law, illegal. However I felt there was just cause and that it really had been in the public interest. I had been honest about what I was doing – I had filmed it! – and letters had been sent to the Home Office, Scotland Yard and the DVLA explaining what I had done and why.

My sole reason for making the programme was to show how easy it was to commit Identity Theft, so that what happened to me wouldn't happen to anyone else. It was ironic that when I had tracked down the thief who had stolen my identity and handed the name and address to the police, nothing was done. Yet when I had done it, without any criminal intent, I had been arrested and was now facing imprisonment.

I was meant to have been away at gigs that weekend, but I cancelled everything. I couldn't face it, and, more importantly, I couldn't face not being with Rosy and the kids. As it was the school summer holidays we had been planning to go away for a few days, probably to Spain. I now didn't want to do this either. I wasn't sure if I was even allowed to leave the country – although, either way, surely the Costa del Sol was the best place to go as I'd no doubt make some like-minded criminal friends.

Over the next couple of days I received calls from Rebecca, Hilary and Sally, who all told me how sorry they were to hear of my arrest. How lovely.

My parents came to visit and asked about the programme. I told them that it didn't have a transmission date yet. I didn't want to tell them what had happened until I knew the outcome. I also wanted as few people to know about this arrest as possible and there was no way my mum could have kept it a secret . . .

I had discovered that, while I was being questioned in the police station, Scotland Yard detectives had raided the production company offices looking for evidence. Fortunately the information they wanted was all there, filed and dated. If we really were all criminal masterminds, at least we were organised ones.

A meeting was arranged for me to chat with an independent lawyer who had been brought in by Channel

4. Hilary, Sally, Jessica, Rebecca and the Channel 4 lawyers also attended the meeting. Paul (the independent lawyer) told me how surprised he had been that this case had gone as far as it had. That was until he'd looked into it further and discovered that Charles Clarke himself had insisted on my arrest.

(I was later to read, in an interview with a newspaper, Mr Clarke had said: 'This matter is now in the hands of the police and I think the only thing to say is that this absolutely proves the need for identity cards.' No. It didn't.)

Paul said that the case would either go to court – where, if found guilty, I could receive a prison sentence – or I might be offered a police caution. This latter option didn't sound too bad at all. Surely a caution, by definition, was just a warning; a yellow card, a slap on the wrist, a 'you've been a very naughty boy, now don't do it again'. Apparently not. I was told that a caution, although not a conviction, has similarities to a criminal record in so much as it will stay with you for a minimum of five years and can affect obtaining anything from credit to car insurance.

They all asked me what I would do if I were offered the caution. I didn't know. Would it be better to have my time in court? Would the Crown Prosecution Service actually let it go that far or would they dismiss it before then? In truth I didn't like either options and thought them both incredibly unjust. I suggested that I write to Charles Clarke personally and explain the situation. Hilary said that if I did want to do that, she would make sure he received the letter by hand. I asked her how she could guarantee this. That's when she, reluctantly, told me – she knew his bodyguard!

THIS is how she knew the route he would take to Parliament! THIS is why she'd said doorstepping him was a bad idea! Because the bodyguard had advised against it. I couldn't believe it. All this time and she'd had access to Charles Clarke. Was this the reason the meetings had been cancelled? Had he known about it all the time, because she had told him?

Paul then told everyone else that they would also be interviewed by the police. Everyone else, that is, excluding the Channel 4 lawyers as they were immune. The lawyers suggested that they everyone just said, 'No comment.' Jessica asked how that would help me, to which one of the lawyers replied, in front of me, 'You can't help Bennett, so just think about yourselves.'

Lovely.

And to think, if I had agreed to accept their initial contract, which stated that I would not be offered legal representation in the unlikely event of anything happening, I would now be paying thousands of pounds for legal advice.

After the meeting I rang friends and friends-of-friends who were lawyers. I also rang the legal departments of the Writer's Guild of Great Britain, and Equity, as I have been a member of both for many years. I wanted to know their opinion on whether I should take the caution – if offered – or go to court. The responses I received differed from 'It'll never go to court, call their bluff' to 'Take the caution and run . . .' I was none the wiser. The only thing they did all agree on was the injustice of the situation.

The following day, as Paul had predicted, the Police interviewed everyone on the production team. I spoke with Jessica that evening and she told me, as advised, that they had all said, 'No comment.' And that was good enough for the police. They were all told, through Paul, that no further action was to be taken against anyone at the production company or Channel 4.

Just against me.

I know that the Channel 4 lawyers had given me all the advice in good faith, after all they hadn't wanted me to get arrested, that wouldn't have been in anyone's best interest, but everything just seemed so unjust.

For the next few days – and nights, as there was no way I could sleep properly – I tried to decide the best course of action. Of course I didn't know for a fact that the police would offer me a caution, but Paul felt it was likely.

I enjoy playing poker, and the thought of bluffing them in the hope that they would drop the charges did appeal. And if I had been single this would have definitely been my decision. But I had a family. I couldn't bear the thought of them having to go through a court trial – however unlikely that might be. So I realised that I had no option; if it were offered, I would have to accept the caution.

Chapter 13

A few nights later I compèred my regular gig at a theatre in Hemel Hempstead. It was one of the oddest nights I'd ever had as a comedian. As usual it was meant to have been me as MC and two acts performing thirty minutes each. However, the first act only did eighteen minutes and the second act . . . didn't turn up. At all. The theatre manager was going to offer the audience their money back when I suggested that, as an alternative, I would ask the audience if they wanted to see my Edinburgh show. They agreed. So I did the show – except, instead of just finishing where I always had, I continued the story. I told a group of strangers what had been going on over the past few months. I told them about the documentary, the arrest . . . everything. They were shocked, appalled, but mostly they were angry. They could not believe what had happened to me. After the gig – which received a fantastic round of applause – there was a queue of people waiting to talk to me more about it. It was incredible. One woman made me very emotional when she said, 'You know, the last act was not *meant* to turn up. You were *meant* to tell us this story.' I know it sounds ridiculous, and really out of character for me, but even as I write this I am getting a cold shiver thinking about it.

The morning after the gig, Paul, the lawyer, rang me and told me that the police were going to offer me a caution – the following day at Harrow Road Police Station. Paul and I had another long conversation in which I went through everything with him again. I just couldn't get the injustice of it all out of my head. He told me that I still didn't have to accept the caution and, even once we were at the station, I could refuse to sign it. I could still call their bluff in the hope that they would say, 'In that case we're dropping the case.' I just didn't know. And neither did he.

I stayed up the whole night looking up everything to do with police cautions. By 6 a.m. I virtually knew the Code of the Crown Prosecution Service off by heart.

I met Paul at Harrow Road Police Station; I was obviously delighted to be back. We were told that the officer who was coming to issue the caution – one of the officers who had come to arrest me at my house – was going to be an hour late. So Paul and I went for a coffee. We had a really good chat and went through everything. Again. He was quite surprised by my knowledge of the proceedings and requirements. I told him that if comedy stops working out I might go into law. He laughed, before informing me that, ironically, getting into law would be difficult if I had a caution. After the coffee we walked around the car park next to the police station. I was still unsure what to do. Paul could only advise me, but, as he said, the final decision would be mine. We once again went over the options. I could accept the caution, thereby admitting guilt and intent and making everyone's life easier – oh, and by 'everyone', I mean the police and all those involved at the production company and Channel 4. Or I could refuse to accept the

112

caution. If I chose that option, then the police might just throw it out or they might take it to the CPS who would probably see that there was no case, that it wasn't done with malice or for any financial gain, and throw it out themselves.

But there was a chance that the police and the CPS would want to make an example of me. That's what Charles Clarke wanted. There was a real possibility that it could go to court and that I'd be found guilty. That could mean a fine, a jail sentence and a criminal record. The one thing Paul did say that gave me some hope was that, because the case dealt with a driving licence, the caution would be listed under the Highways/Road Traffic Act. Although it was still a caution, and one I would apparently have to declare for many years, it wasn't as serious an offence as 'Fraud', which is what the police had initially wanted. Paul said this was quite significant. I trusted him and hoped that, even though he had been hired by Channel 4, he genuinely was on my side.

We eventually went to the station and met one of the officers who had arrested me. He smiled, shook my hand and asked me how I was.

'Well, because of what you and your colleagues did to me, my life is in turmoil, I can't sleep, my wife is constantly upset and I don't know what long-term effects this is all going to have,' is what I wanted to say. However, I just said, 'Fine, thanks.'

We were taken into a small upstairs room and there he officially offered me the caution. I picked up the pen and then hesitated. I thought again, 'Why should I accept this? Why should everyone else get away with it? Why should

I let myself be the scapegoat? Why isn't Channel 4 being cautioned? Or Sally? Or Jessica? Or Rebecca? Or Hilary? Should I turn it down? Should I throw it back in their faces and to hell with the consequences?' I looked at Paul. I looked back down at the paper in front of me. I then made my decision . . .

Ten minutes later, Paul and I were walking back to the car park in silence. We stopped next to Paul's car.

'Do you think it was the right decision?'

Paul looked at me and shrugged. 'I think so. But the truth is, we'll never know.'

We shook hands and I thanked him for everything he had done. He told me to contact him if he ever needed a lawyer. I thanked him and told him that I planned on never calling him again. He smiled, got into his car and drove off. I then walked over to my own car, opened the door and sat inside. I looked at the police sign outside the station. I remember the respect I always had for the police when I was a child . We all did. A police officer once came to my primary school and we all sat there open-mouthed in awe as he stood on the stage at assembly and spoke to us. The atmosphere was spoilt slightly however when, towards the end of the Q&A, a boy in the top year put his hand up and said, 'Can you arrest anyone with your hat off?'

Now, here I was, an adult, feeling all the respect I once had flowing away. Yes, they had been doing their job, but 'just following orders' should never be a justification.

After I had signed the caution, the arresting officer had said, 'I really didn't think you'd sign it.' To this day I don't know what that meant. Did he mean he was expecting to have to rip it up and throw the whole case out or did he mean that he thought I would take my chance in court? I don't know and I never will. As I was leaving the office, he asked me if I would tell him when I was next gigging in London, as he'd like to come along with some mates. Well, I had seen him at work, so to him it must have seemed fair.

Driving back from the police station I had mixed emotions. There was a feeling of relief that I had made a decision – even if I wasn't sure whether or not it had been the right one – but there was still also the incredible sense of injustice. But at least it was now all over. And then I remembered we had planned to go to Wales the following week to see my parents. I would have to tell them what had happened. I thought about driving back to the police station . . .

Chapter 14

Despite having to reveal everything to my parents, our time in Wales was very relaxing. I needed a break. When I told them what had happened my mum asked me why I hadn't told them before. She then went to bed with a headache – which sort of answered the question. Dad, as always, was logical and rational. He just wanted to make sure there would be no further repercussions that would affect me. I told him that, in truth, I didn't know, but I hoped there wouldn't be. While I was there I received a call from Rebecca, who wanted to organise a meeting to discuss how we could incorporate what had happened into the documentary. I was delighted about this. First of all it meant that Channel 4 still wanted to transmit it – I had been worried that in light of everything that had happened they would cancel the transmission – and secondly it meant I could now talk about the arrest in the programme and add scenes to show the unfairness of it all. Maybe I could get a quote from Charles Clarke himself. He had already been interviewed in the press about it. Maybe he would now meet me face to face . . .

Two days after returning from Wales I had lunch with Rebecca. It was the most rushed and unrelaxed lunch I've ever had. She arrived late, said that she didn't want to eat and told me to quickly order. While she waited, impatiently, for my food to arrive she told me that she was sorry about what happened to me and that Channel 4 was prepared to offer me some money as compensation. I was completely taken aback by this. She explained that this was what they paid to journalists who suffer consequences in 'the line of duty'. To me it seemed like scapegoat money. (Incidentally this was fractionally more money than I had been paid for actually making the programme. For dedicating a year and a half of my life to make the documentary, I had been paid only £1,500!) Rebecca and I then, briefly, discussed the scenes I planned to shoot. I told her that I wanted to film myself talking to camera outside Harrow Road Police Station, explaining what had happened. She agreed. I also said that I wanted to re-edit some of the earlier scenes to make it more relevant to the ending. She told me that none of the other directors had re-edited theirs. I explained that none of the other directors had been arrested. Then, as my food arrived, I told her that I didn't want to work with Sally again. She was surprised by this – which in itself surprised me. Surely she was aware we didn't get on. This wasn't discussed further as she started receiving and then replying to messages on her phone. She then told me she had to leave. She paid the bill and then said I could finish on my own. I said that I suddenly wasn't that hungry and so I left with her. I have never left that much food on my plate. I'm glad my mum wasn't there to see it.

The next day I had a call from Hilary, who told me that she would be sending me a shooting schedule for the scenes to be filmed outside the police station. I was very pleased. Rebecca had obviously spoken with her about it. That day I received some more good news. A publisher had heard about my Edinburgh show and wanted to know if I planned to write a book on the subject. I hadn't – until then.

A couple of days later I had a meeting with him and he talked about an advance. I had ALWAYS wanted to have a book published and suddenly all the awful things that had happened over the past year seemed to be for a reason. I was incredibly excited. The only problem was, as well as publishing my book, he also wanted to represent me as an agent. Although I already had an agent for television and film writing, they didn't cover books. However, although I realised that I needed a book agent, I was slightly worried that this would be a conflict of interest. How do you negotiate with yourself? And how would I know I was receiving a good deal? I suggested that I find myself a separate book agent and that they would deal with him as the publisher. He was less keen, but he agreed.

Never having dealt in this world before, I spoke to various friends and asked for their opinions. Lee, one of the other writers on *Genie in the House*, was very friendly with a well-respected agent. I met with her and her assistant and she seemed very interested. Of course, who wouldn't be interested when you're approached by a client who has already, at least in theory, been commissioned?! The agent asked me if I planned on writing any other books. I told her about a fiction novel on which I had been working off and on for the previous year or so – whenever I'd had free time between gigging, filming and being arrested. She asked to see what I had written so far. I was quite nervous about this as no one had read it and, well, I didn't know if it was any good. I knew that I could write scripts, but this was completely new for me. It felt like showing someone your personal diary or a home-made adult video (no, I haven't!). Anyway, I agreed to send it to her.

I had been writing for the children's TV series *The Slammer* and that evening I took Yasmin to a recording of the programme in east London. She loved it and enjoyed meeting the cast afterwards. She even beat one of the main actors at pool in the green room – which he wasn't happy about. With everything that had been going on, I'd forgotten how lucky I am to be doing the job I do and how exciting it can be for my children.

A couple of days later the agent rang me and told me she loved what I had written of the book so far. I was really pleased. Perhaps I could write a book after all. She then told me that she planned on asking the publisher for a two-book deal. A two-book deal! I hadn't thought anyone would ever be interested in a book; now I was potentially looking at producing two of them.

An hour after this call, I had a call from the publisher himself. He wasn't happy. Initially I thought it was because I had decided to sign with another agent instead of him, or even because she'd asked for this two-book deal. But it wasn't that at all. He was unhappy with my choice of agent. Unbeknown to me, they'd had a big falling-out over a book written by one of her clients. Of all the agents for me to choose! He told me that he would still look at what I had sent him – a brief synopsis of the Identity Theft book together with chapter outlines – and that he would, somewhat reluctantly, get back to my agent.

Just as this book deal looked to be falling apart before it had even started, I received a call from Hilary. Channel 4 had decided that shooting more scenes was too expensive. That I had saved them a fortune by not taking the case to court was apparently irrelevant. They had decided that they wanted to put a brief 'caption' at the end instead.

I couldn't believe it.

This was my opportunity to show the complete injustice of what had happened, yet they wanted to sum it all up in a caption! I was incredibly disappointed. Two hours after this phone call, Hilary called me again. The Channel 4 lawyers were now having serious doubts as to whether the programme should air at all. They were worried that people might see it as way to steal someone's identity and that Channel 4 would be accused of being an accessory to a crime. Yes, feel free to reread that. An accessory to a crime.

I used to enjoy the programme *ER*, yet I never came away from it thinking I was now able to perform a heart transplant. So, after everything, it looked like the programme on which I had been working for the previous year and half, the one which had led to my arrest, might not ever be seen.

Chapter 15

How Not to Lose Your Identity.

This was the new title of the programme. I hated it. It made no sense. It was a negative phrase. My title had been '*How to Steal an Identity*'. I had chosen this title as the programme was about . . . how to steal an identity. Genius. However, the Channel 4 lawyers had said that if the programme were to be shown, and that was still uncertain, then this would have to be the title. They were worried about repercussions from Ofcom, as it could look like an instruction video. Even though the content was to remain the same, they felt that this title would have no repercussions on them. I tried to explain that I hadn't shown how I managed to obtain the driving licence, and that bin-raiding is a known crime whereby, as misleading as it sounds, you raid someone's bins! But it didn't matter. There was nothing I could do about it. That was the title.

Also, unbeknown to me, Rebecca had told Hilary that she didn't even want the captions as it would be time-consuming to make and unnecessary. Fortunately Hilary had argued my case for me, explaining to Rebecca that she felt it was the least they could do . . .

Eventually it was decided that the programme would

be transmitted. I was delighted. It wouldn't all be going to waste.

The new date and time was 15 May at 11 p.m. It wasn't 'prime time', but at least it wasn't the original scheduled time of 1 a.m.

I now had four weeks in which to garner as much interest as I could through press and publicity. The Channel 4 press office said they would help, but I had now learned not to rely on anyone. So I also contacted the press myself.

I was interviewed by several publications and booked for some guest spots on radio and TV. Annoyingly the newspaper which had interviewed Charles Clarke over the matter, stated that I wouldn't allow them to interview me as I had agreed to sell my story exclusively to a 'downmarket tabloid'. This wasn't true at all and gave me my first personal glimpse into how things can be manipulated by the press.

A few days before the programme was due to go out, Rosy and I were in a newsagent's looking for an eighth birthday card for Yasmin. While there, I saw that the new editions of the *TV Times* and *Radio Times* had come out – the ones that would cover the transmission date of the programme. I tentatively opened the magazines and turned to 15 May. There, in the *TV Times*, staring back at me, was . . . me. A photo of me, which Jessica had taken with my camera at the shopping centre in Swansea, was printed in the magazine. Next to it was the heading 'Pick of The Day: How Not to Lose Your Identity'.

Pick of the Day!!!

There was also review of the programme which

described it as 'fascinating and disturbing'. I thought I was going to explode with excitement. I ran over to Rosy and showed her. She was even more excited than me.

Ever since I had decided to attempt a career as a thespian, I had dreamed of being in these TV listings magazines. And there I was. I went through the other TV guides as well and I was in ALL of them. There were photos and great reviews. I bought three copies of each.

Later that afternoon, possibly as a result of the good reviews, I had a call from the Channel 4 press office. The *Lorraine* programme had been in touch with them and wanted to interview me on the morning of the day of transmission. I was delighted, even though I knew I'd now worry about what I was going to wear . . .

The big day eventually arrived and I'd hardly slept. So no change there. A car came for me at 6 a.m. to take me to the *Lorraine* studios. I was taken into the green room and introduced to Owen Roberts, who would also be appearing on the programme. He worked for the credit reference agency Call Credit, and was there to give facts and figures about Identity Theft. (He and I immediately bonded over our shared interest in ID theft, data protection and comic books. We remain good friends to this day.)

After hair and make-up (mainly make-up in my case) we were taken to the studio floor and introduced to Lorraine. The interview then started and they showed a clip of the programme – and I was appalled to see that I was wearing the same shirt! I tried to explain that I had lost so much money from the ID theft that I had little left over to buy new clothes...

I felt the interview went well and I received several

complimentary text messages in the car on the way back.

Once I'd arrived home I sent out hundreds of emails to producers, casting directors, acting agents, school careers officers, etc., letting them know that the programme was on. I didn't know if it would make any difference but I wanted to take full advantage of the fact that I was about to be on TV.

I still wasn't 100 per cent sure that the programme would actually be transmitted at all. Yes, it was in all the listings publications and, yes, I had been promoting it, but I couldn't help feeling that someone at Channel 4 would decide it wasn't a good idea after all and cancel it at the last minute.

At 10.30, Rosy and I sat down to wait for it to come on. We watched the programme before it – I have no idea what that was – and saw my programme being trailed in the ad break. I was as nervous as I was excited.

From the moment the programme started until the end credits, I cried. Then my parents rang to say how much they enjoyed it – and I cried again. I don't know why. I think it was the release of the build-up of tension/ worry/exhaustion of the previous eighteen months.

The caption at the end stated that I had been arrested and received a caution. Unfortunately it didn't say: 'However, no one else was in any way punished and so they are all free to just get on with their lives . . .'

In a normal day I usually receive one or possibly two hits on my website. In the two hours following the programme I received over 2000 hits before my website crashed!

The following morning I read reviews of the programme

in the press. They were all very complimentary and the *Guardian* and the *Telegraph* had chosen the programme as their 'Pick of the Day'. The only paper to criticise it was the *Daily Express* which thought the whole thing had been set up. Ah well.

That afternoon I went to the dentist. He had seen the programme and was also very complimentary. He asked me several questions about the making of it. Unfortunately I was unable to answer anything, mainly as his hands were in my mouth. After leaving the dentist I went to a local mobile-phone shop to see about upgrading my phone – and the guy in the shop recognised me! It wasn't world-wide fame, but it did feel good.

This recognition occurred again two nights later when I was performing at a gig in Birmingham. Halfway through my set, someone shouted out, 'Are you Charles Clarke?' to which another audience member responded with 'No, he's Spider-Man.'

Unfortunately, although I was delighted with the reference, most of the audience were completely bemused and I ended up diverting from my set to explain what was going on. It didn't make for the best of gigs, and I realised I'd have to write some material to cover it in case it ever happened again.

Unsurprisingly, following the transmission of the programme, no one at either the production company or Channel 4 contacted me. There was no 'Well done', or 'We've had great feedback'. Nothing. I had written to Rebecca to ask what the viewing figures were. I'd received no reply. I think they were all grateful to see the back of both me and the programme.

The book publisher had asked me to write between 4,000 and 5,000 words, just to see my style of writing. I was happy to do it – even though he had only given me two weeks. Over the next few days I worked flat out on the book during the day and gigged in the evenings. I didn't want to let this opportunity pass me by, but I also needed to earn money. By the end of the two weeks I was exhausted but pleased with what I had written.

A few days after sending the 4,820 words to the publisher, I received this from him via my new book agent:

> . . . *Thanks for letting me see Bennett's Identity Theft book. It's good. He writes well. He has timing and a nice, funny turn of phrase . . . But, sadly, it's not for us . . . Do give my best to Bennett and wish him luck.*

Crap!

He had gone from interest and excitement in the book, to . . . this. Why? Was it because of the two-book deal? Was it because I hadn't let him represent me? Or was it his past relationship with my new agent? Whatever it was, that chapter had apparently ended . . .

Chapter 16

Over the next couple of months things started getting back to normal. The buzz around the programme slowly started to fade away and the national newspapers chose their next 'Pick of the Day'.

I was still receiving the occasional complimentary email as well as some quite odd ones. For example a woman wrote to me telling me how much she'd enjoyed the programme and then asked if I could help her son escape from prison. I'm not sure how much of the programme she had actually watched. I was also asked to appear on several radio shows and news programmes. Each time this happened I asked them to put 'Comedian' in the caption. However they always put 'Identity Theft Victim'. This was of course true, and the reason I was there, but it wasn't going to help my stand-up career. On one of the news programmes they wrote: 'Aaron Benett, Identity Theft Victim'. Which was ironic.

Also, as a result of the programme, I had been asked to speak at a number of corporate events around the country. I was now incorporating the experience of making the documentary, and of being arrested, into the show. I had added some slides and showed the video clip of the shopping centre scam. The show had also become a little more interactive as I started asking the audience whether any of them had ever been arrested. Some of the stories were fantastic. On one occasion someone put their hand up and said, 'Yes, I have.' I asked him why, and he said, 'For stealing a pint glass from a pub.' This met with some surprise from myself and the other audience members until his friend sitting next to him added, '. . . and smashing it over someone's head!'

On another occasion I asked the question and at first there was no response. I was about to continue when a man put his hand up and said, 'I've been arrested.' His wife then turned to him and said, 'No, you haven't.' The room fell silent as he turned to her and said, 'Yes, I have.' 'What for?' she asked. 'For running an illegal lottery ring,' he replied. 'No, I know about that,' she said. 'But that wasn't you, that was your brother.'

There was a pause and the man then said, 'Er . . . we did it together. And you know when he and I went away on holiday last year for two weeks to Tenerife and I had my phone stolen? Well, that wasn't true. We were both inside.'

I stood on the stage, thinking, 'Well, this is awkward.'

The wife stood up and, in floods of tears, ran from the room.

The man stood up and started to follow her. He then stopped, turned, angrily pointed at me and said, 'You shouldn't have asked!'

There was another time when I performed the show to the management of a large company and asked the question. A woman in a very high position in the company put up her hand and then immediately changed her mind and put it down again. So I just left this and moved on. I'm kidding. I of course pursued this, as did her colleagues. She eventually admitted to having been arrested for drunkenly urinating in the street. Everyone was shocked and, instead of laughing, the room fell silent. Fortunately the MD of the company eventually started laughing and everyone then joined in. I think she kept her job.

I was pleased with all the new material I had written about the events. Little did I know there was about to be even more . . .

The children had both moved up a year at primary school and a letter had been sent home asking if any parents would volunteer to listen to children reading. As I missed teaching, I thought it would be a great thing to do. So I applied.

When I had accepted the police caution it had been under the 1988 Road Traffic Act as it concerned the procuring of a driving licence. They had wanted to caution me under 'Fraud', but they knew I wouldn't have accepted that, as it was a much more serious offence with more damaging implications.

When I applied to teach at the children's school, I naturally, and quite correctly, had to be checked by the Criminal Records Bureau. I assumed there wouldn't be any problem.

I was wrong.

I had a phone call from the school office asking me if I would go in to see the head teacher. Waiting outside her office I felt like I was back at school myself, although this time the chairs were a lot smaller. The head had seen the documentary and had told me she'd enjoyed it and thought I looked quite thin in it . . . (You'll have to have read

Chapter 12 to get that reference.) She therefore knew all about the arrest and was surprised that it had flagged up on the CRB check.

So was I. It just didn't seem relevant.

According to the guidelines, she had to ask me a series of questions. These included things like 'Will you reoffend?' and 'Do you regret your actions'? She also had to write down whether she felt I was a risk to the public, whether I would have direct contact with vulnerable people and what would be the nature of the contact with the children. It was awful. We both felt uncomfortable.

We both then had to sign the document, before sending it off to be assessed. Before signing, I briefly looked over it – and I could not believe what I saw.

As I mentioned, the police had wanted to caution me under the 1968 Theft Act for 'Obtaining Property by Deception'. Or 'Fraud'. But I had stated that I wouldn't sign that as there was no deception and it wasn't theft. They had reluctantly agreed, which is why I was offered the caution under the Road Traffic Act instead. However, as I signed the declaration I could see the details of the caution. It read that I had been cautioned for 'Obtaining Property by Deception'.

As soon as I arrived home I contacted Paul, the lawyer who had helped me. We hadn't been in touch for a long time and he probably thought he'd seen the back of me and my case. However, he was as shocked and angry as I was when I told him what I had seen. He said he would look into it immediately.

A few days later he came back to me. And he sounded even more appalled. Apparently, after I had accepted and signed the caution, the police had changed it! They had removed the Road Traffic Act and replaced it with the Theft Act, under the heading 'Obtaining Property by Deception.' They had changed it, so that it now stated I had been cautioned for Fraud. Which, ironically, was fraud.

I would have to find a way to have this changed back. As this was nothing to do with the actual case, i.e. not directly associated with Channel 4, I would have to pay for this myself. And I knew it wouldn't be cheap. Fortunately Paul said that he would deal with it, for no charge, as he was very angry about it himself, and he'd been with me when I'd signed the caution. I was delighted and grateful.

Paul told me that I had to fill in a Data Protection Act Complaint Form, stating what the problem was and asking to have it changed on the Police National Computer database as well as with the Criminal Records Bureau. Once this was completed, he would send it in.

As is usual with such things, there was a substantial amount of paperwork. They probably hope that people will give up and not bother making a complaint. It was incredibly time-consuming, but I had to do it; I was too shocked and upset not to.

Weeks, then months, passed as I waited for a reply. I was gigging quite a lot, which I hoped, in theory, would take my mind off things. That December I actually performed twenty-six gigs. They were all great except two. One of these was at a club in Camden, where I died as I have never died before. And, to make things worse, Rosy was there to witness it. I could make excuses – for example, I was the second act on and the compère hadn't mentioned that there would be two acts in the first half, so everyone had gone to the bar/toilet/out for a cigarette as I was walking to the stage. But, whatever the reason, I did badly. The other was down to an anti-Semitic audience in Edinburgh.

It was a full crowd, all office Christmas parties, and my set had been going well; big laughs and the occasional round of applause. Then, around ten minutes in, it suddenly stopped. I had to address it and asked the audience what had happened. 'It's because you're a Jew!' came the response. This received a round of applause larger than any of the ones I'd had. I usually mention I'm Jewish and Welsh right at the start of my set, but because something had happened at the bar as I walked to the stage, I'd started making jokes about this and so my 'revelation' came much later.

This unpleasant remark was followed by several anti-Semitic heckles, most of which met with laughter and/or applause. I realised that I wasn't going to win this. So I walked off.

'Where are you going now? Back to the synagogue?!'

I left the venue to laughter, none of which I had intentionally caused. In all my years of performing as a comedian, this had never happened before. It was horrible.

Arriving home after that awful weekend, I checked through my post hoping there would be something from the Criminal Records Bureau. Or at least a basket of fruit and an apology from the police. There was neither. What I did receive however was a notification that BAFTA, of which I've been a member since winning a writing award, was accepting submissions for their prestigious television awards. There was a category called 'Single Documentary'.

I was curious to know if my programme was eligible. I looked through the criteria and could see that *How to Steal an Identity* (that was the real title as far as I was concerned) did fit the criteria.

The following day I contacted both Channel 4 and the production company – neither of which I had heard from in months – and asked them which one of them would be interested in submitting the programme. Once I had reminded them who I was, and to which programme I was referring, they both told me that they weren't at all interested. The production company told me that they only submitted programmes they believed had any chance of success. Nice.

So, after working so hard to keep most of the elements I wanted in the programme, struggling to compromise with the editing and being arrested for making it, I was the only one who seemed to have any belief in the programme's merits. I therefore decided to enter it myself at a cost of £250.

Once my application had been accepted I was given the list of BAFTA members so that I could contact them and ask them to vote for the programme. I also offered a DVD copy to anyone who hadn't seen it.

I was hoping most of them had already seen it as I was going to have to pay for each copy and post them out myself . . .

Over the next couple of weeks I received incredible feedback. Many voting members had seen it and liked it. I was so pleased. I hoped they would also vote for it.

On 21 January 1998 I had a call from BAFTA telling me that the programme had been shortlisted. I was now, officially, a BAFTA-shortlisted director! The person who rang me told me that the response to the programme had been great and that she felt there was every chance it would be nominated.

Nominated!!

That night we all went out to celebrate. Of course I didn't have too late a night as I wanted to get up early and work on my acceptance speech . . .

The following day the production company contacted me. They had heard about the programme being shortlisted and said that they would reimburse me the money I had spent on entering it for BAFTA. Unbelievable! The programme in which they had no interest could win an award. And now they wanted a part of it.

I told them that I was happy paying for it myself, as I was proud of the programme before it had been shortlisted.

There had still been no response from the CRB about my enquiry into their 'mistake'. Paul had contacted them via post and phone calls, but they hadn't come back to either of us.

Then, months later, they did.

They wrote and told us that no complaint form had been sent in! They didn't say that they might have mislaid it; they said that no form had been sent in! I'd like to say that I couldn't believe it, but in truth, after everything that had happened, I quite easily believed it. I assumed this was another tactic to stop people from pursuing any claim. Their letter stated that, if they didn't hear anything within the next ten days, then they would consider the case closed and my record would remain as it was.

Paul, who was furious on my behalf, contacted them

and had the new form sent over immediately. It was signed for and a confirmation letter received. Now I just had to wait. Again.

This disappointment was followed by another a few days later when I was informed by BAFTA that the programme hadn't been nominated. As well as being disappointed, I was, without wanting to sound cocky, a little surprised. I knew there had been great feedback, and many people had told me that they would be voting for it – even though they weren't meant to give me that information.

I spoke about this to a contact I had at BAFTA. She told me, in confidence, that she believed there had been influence on the decision from elsewhere. I asked her what she meant by this, and she implied that some people didn't want the current government to be seen in a bad light.

Really? Was that true? Surely that wouldn't/couldn't have influenced, or even altered, the voting? I didn't believe it, and I still don't, but it was an odd thing to say.

So that was that. The programme had been on, it had been critically praised and my parents had been recognised in the street – which made them incredibly proud. And it had been shortlisted by BAFTA. I was very pleased with what I had done.

I would now return to gigging and writing.

I had been asked to write a feature film of *Genie in the House*. Although I had once written a film script on spec (unfortunately it was about film extras and I had finished it three months before Ricky Gervais started his television series on the subject), I had never been paid to write one. It was both daunting and exciting. It was to be set in Paris, so I went over there for brainstorming sessions with the producer and other writers – just to have a look around and get ideas. While I was in Paris I received an email from someone in Poland. They had seen the documentary and wanted to know if I would be interested in speaking at their 'International Congress on Internal Control, Internal Audit, Anticorruption and Anti-Fraud Issues'. It wasn't the catchiest of titles, but I was delighted to be asked. Also, it was taking place in Krakow, a place I had always wanted to visit.

As with Italy, I would have liked to take the family with me. Unfortunately, as this event was taking place during school time, I wasn't able to. In retrospect that was no bad thing, as the children had never seen me drunk . . .

Let me explain.

That trip to Poland was memorable for several reasons. Firstly, as there were very few English-speaking delegates in attendance, my talk/performance had to be translated via headphones. Comedy doesn't lend itself well to this, and it really threw off my timing. For example, I would say something potentially amusing and the few English-speaking people would laugh. It would then be translated into Polish and I'd have to wait for the Polish-speaking people to laugh. The only problem was, I couldn't hear the translator – who was a fantastic guy with the best moustache I have ever seen – so I didn't know if he was still translating or if he had finished and they just hadn't found it funny. Sometimes I would move on to the next bit and then get the previous laugh, or otherwise wait an uncomfortably long time for a laugh which never transpired. Despite that, the talk went well and my Q&A which followed was interesting, especially as one person asked me if I was really Jewish.

Of my whole Identity Theft story, that really would have been the oddest part to have made up!

Speaking of being Jewish, the next reason for this trip being so memorable was that I spent the day after the conference in Auschwitz.

I had always wanted to visit Auschwitz. Well 'wanted to' is probably the wrong expression. I always felt I 'should'. I knew it would be traumatic and upsetting, so I attempted to prepare myself. But I soon discovered that was impossible. To get to the concentration camp I had to catch a bus from the centre of Krakow. It was an old bus with broken windows and no suspension. It was a two-hour journey, most of which was along a bumpy dirt track. I would normally have complained, but knowing how others had once journeyed there put things into perspective. That and the knowledge that I at least had a return ticket.

From the moment I walked through the iconic gates and looked up at the imposing barbed-wire-swathed lookout tower, I felt sick, angry and, of course, incredibly upset. The things I saw – the glass cabinets full of toys, shoes and, worst of all, women's and girls' hair – will stay with me forever. I can't come to terms with the fact that this is something that happened during my parents' lifetime.

I know school visits are organised to the camps, and I am all for that. It is something that obviously must never ever be forgotten.

I had heard what I thought to be an urban myth, that birds don't fly over the camp. However, as I was leaving,

I saw a flock of birds flying towards it. They then swooped down, pecked at the grass in front of the gates, took off and flew back the way they had come. It was powerful and eerie.

The bus on the way there had been full and quite noisy from all the people talking. It was also full going back, but this time it was silent.

That night I had been invited to dinner with all three hundred of the delegates from the conference. We were taken to a beautiful Polish restaurant where I had traditional Polish food, or at least a vegetarian version, which isn't traditional at all – as they continually pointed out. Before the meal started the organiser called up several people to receive an award. I clapped even though I couldn't understand what they were receiving or why they were receiving it. I then heard my name. I walked up, assuming, as has happened when I've done these things in the past, that I would be given a certificate or something. However, the organiser said something in Polish and then handed me the microphone. I stood there, confused, while three hundred people stared. My wonderfully moustached interpreter then explained to me that I would now be doing some jokes. I thanked them for the offer, politely shook my head and attempted to hand back the microphone. They looked horrified. Apparently this was a huge insult. I didn't know what to do. Apart from anything else my day in Auschwitz obviously hadn't put me in the right frame of mind for performing comedy. I quickly went through my material in my head. They'd heard my Identity Theft show and I couldn't think of any of my 'normal' set that would translate. So I told a joke. A traditional joke. About a rabbi and a prostitute. No, I don't know why either. Needless to say it fell flat. I don't know if it was the joke, the translation or just me. Whatever it was it didn't work. I sat down to looks of dismay and confusion. Ah well, I thought, the evening can't get worse.

I was wrong.

The tables had bottles of frozen vodka on them and everyone had a glass, which was apparently a shot glass though they were much larger than normal shot glasses. In fact I have seen smaller vases. Despite my awful joke, as the first course arrived, people came up to me to thank me for the talk I had given the previous day and to share a drink. I accepted a couple of these but soon realised, as I hadn't eaten yet, I'd perhaps best not drink any more. So when the next person came up, thanked me and offered me a drink, I thanked them but politely declined. Oh dear. This was worse than saying 'no' to being handed the microphone earlier. It was like one of those old Western films when the piano player stops and everyone turns to look at the 'stranger' who's just walked in.

So I drank.

I'll be honest, I wasn't feeling drunk at all. Just quite warm. However, when I got up to go to the loo – mainly to avoid being asked to drink any more – I discovered a problem. I couldn't feel my legs. I'm not medically trained, despite watching all those episodes of ER, but I knew this wasn't normal. I literally had to lift my legs off the chair, and slowly slide my feet as best I could towards the toilet. I came back to my seat to discover my first course had arrived – and was currently being stared at by my meat-eating companions. I started to take a mouthful of the food and then I felt a weird feeling. The warmth I had felt earlier was now turning to real heat. This started at my legs and then worked its way upwards. Within moments my whole body felt like I'd been sitting too close to a fire. This was followed by a sudden realisation. I was drunk. Not just drunk but drunker than I had ever been, and I've been drinking since I was sixteen. The room spun; the people looked like Dali clocks. I turned to my melting host and told him that I had to get back to the hotel. He told me that I hadn't eaten anything yet and that there would be dancing later. I explained that I would be unable to do either.

I won't go into details but, suffice to say, on arrival back at my hotel I was a tad poorly. I had to fly back early the following morning and I didn't think I'd make it. I don't know how I managed to pack, get to the airport and check in. Sitting in the plane, perspiring profusely, waiting for it to take off so that I could spend the whole flight in the toilet, wasn't much fun.

For the next week I was ill. Really ill. I later found out through a Polish friend of mine that this particular vodka is one of the strongest there is and that my reaction to it was not uncommon. In fact it's believed that the term 'legless' comes from this reaction. I did not drink alcohol for three months after this experience and I have not touched vodka since.

Not long after returning from Poland I was travelling again. This time to Paris, to perform in the film I had written for *Genie in the House* called 'Legend of the Dragon'. I was to play the part of a magician called the Great Enchanto.

I remember coming up with this name while working through the script on a packed train coming home from a Christmas gig in central London. I was writing on a notepad and constantly had friendly drunken revellers asking me what I was doing.

One of the scenes I wrote described a shot of a row of marquees in front of the Eiffel Tower. Now, here I was, at 7 o'clock in the morning, looking at a row of marquees in front of the Eiffel Tower. It was one of the most exciting feelings I've ever had as a writer. At the time I didn't know I'd be performing in it as well; it just so happened that the actor who was cast in the part could no longer do it. So I volunteered myself. Of course, once I knew I had the part, I accidentally added a few more lines in the rewrite . . .

The time in Paris was fantastic, especially as the family came with me. They also came to the wrap party, where they entertained the cast by telling jokes and dancing. It was great fun – even though I wasn't drinking!

In all this time I still hadn't heard back from the Criminal Records Bureau, despite Paul chasing the complaint. The only thing they had said was that they couldn't act until they had received a report from the police. And the police hadn't responded. Unsurprisingly. Still, at least this time they had acknowledged receipt.

Over the next few weeks I performed my Identity Theft show to various companies around the country. On one day I performed it four times for the same company – different audiences obviously. I even did a show for my local Neighbourhood Watch group, which reminded me of a joke I used to have in my set: 'We had a neighbourhood watch back home – it was my job to wind it.' Brilliant.

I had now added what was happening with the CRB into the show. I was pleased that the audiences were as angry as I was. After one corporate event a man came over to me and, quietly, introduced himself as a senior officer from the Metropolitan Police. He apologised for what had happened and said he would look into it on my behalf. He also told me that it would take a long time to have it changed – if at all. It was basically my word against that of the police. I pointed out that the lawyer had also been present and that he had paperwork which showed what I had been prepared to accept. He said that 'might' help in my favour, but there were no guarantees as this happened more than people imagined.

What a situation . . .

In between chasing the police – yes, I know it's normally the other way around – doing gigs and performing my Identity Theft show, I had managed to finish writing my first ever novel – a romantic comedy. Everyone at my book agency loved it and they immediately sent it out to large publishing houses. I was incredibly excited.

In addition to this, I had received a call from Ricky Gervais asking if I would be the support act for some of his warm-up tour shows. I'd agreed before he'd finished asking.

I always thought it was only bad things that came in threes, but when a highly respected television comedy commissioner, commissioned Robin Ince and me to write a sitcom script, I realised it might be good things too.

It looked as if things were all about to take a turn for the better . . .

Chapter 17

At this time, things were happening in the world that didn't affect me directly but are still worth mentioning; Barack Obama was elected as President of the United States, we had a new coalition government in the UK, and an 'ash cloud' from Iceland caused air-traffic chaos.

On a more personal note, the shows with Ricky Gervais had been going really well. I'd been incredibly nervous at the first one, but they were such a lovely audience and he had given me such a great introduction that I felt relaxed after my opening couple of jokes.

I took my family to one of the shows and introduced them to him. Rosy was surprised at how shy he was, Yasmin thanked him for the signed box set of *Flanimals* he had sent her a couple of years earlier and Xander shook his hand and then went back to playing on his Nintendo.

Robin and I had a meeting with the well-respected comedy commissioner. He told us about his idea for the sitcom and we discussed the situation, plots, characters, etc. We were all happy with it and over the next few weeks Robin and I wrote the first draft. We didn't always agree on everything, but we had enjoyed working together and were both pleased with the finished product. We sent it off and were subsequently called in for a meeting. The commissioner told us that he really liked it. A lot. He then asked us if we could slightly change the main character. Doing as we were told, we changed the main character according to his notes and sent in a new draft. We were called in for another meeting. The commissioner told us that he really liked it. A lot. He then asked us if we could slightly change the plot line.

This went on for weeks, with him telling us how much he liked each draft, a lot, yet also wanting some *slight* changes. We made all the changes accordingly.

Then we had the last meeting.

In this last meeting, the well-respected commissioner said, 'I'm sorry but I don't like this any more. I don't know what's happened to it, but it's completely different to what we started with.'

I showed him all his notes and said that we had worked through them accordingly. The well-respected commissioner then said, 'Well, perhaps you shouldn't have listened to me.'

So that was that. Disappointing and time-consuming.

That same day, just as I was feeling pretty low, I was forwarded an email that my book agent had received from a large publishing house. They loved the book. They thought the writing was funny and loved the characters. However, they wouldn't publish it because . . . wait for it . . . it was written by a man.

Yes.

They felt no one would buy a romantic comedy that had been produced by a male writer. I was a tad annoyed. If they had just said that they didn't like it, fine. But this just seemed incredible. Over the next few weeks I received almost identical responses from other publishers. They all said how much they liked it and how much they had laughed, but then followed this up with: 'Unfortunately as you are a male writer, we wouldn't be able to publish it . . .'

Some of them admitted that there were *some* male writers in this genre but they were few and far between and they were established. I tried to point out that they weren't established until someone had published their books, but there seemed little point.

On this same day, just to prove the rule of three, I met for a coffee with Jessica. I hadn't spoken to her since the day the police questioned them all. She told me that she was really sorry for what had happened and that she had wanted to call me but hadn't known what to say. I told her not to worry. We then chatted about the programme and the consequences of making it. During the conversation I mentioned how surprised I'd been that no one had replied to the letters Sally had sent out explaining what I had done and why I had done it. Instead, I had simply been arrested. Jessica didn't respond. She just looked down at her coffee. I suddenly realised what had happened.

'They were never posted were they?'

'I'm not sure if they were ever posted, but I know they weren't posted at the time. Sally was worried that they might try and stop the programme if they received the letters.'

Well, that explained a lot.

That night I thought about contacting Sally about all this but realised there was little point.

So putting this and the book deal behind me, and while still waiting for a response about the CRB, I decided I would try to focus more on my stand-up.

I had been asked by a production company/comedy

agency if I would be interested in auditioning for the programme *Michael McIntyre's Comedy Roadshow*. I didn't know that they actually held 'auditions'; I assumed they saw you at a gig and if they thought you were good enough then just put you on the programme. But apparently not. They were holding audition shows at the Comedy Store in London, a club I had played at the start of my career. I was delighted to have been offered the opportunity and knew that being one of the comedians on the programme would be a huge career step.

They had told me that I should perform my best eight to ten minutes, so I worked hard at choosing my material and polishing it.

The night of the audition was pretty nerve-wracking. I had been told that the worst spot on the bill was going on at the beginning. So you can imagine my delight when I arrived at the venue to see that I was to be the first act on. Michael, whom I have known since he first started and with whom I had shared many a coffee/lunch at cities around the country, was hosting the evening himself.

Backstage he wished us all luck – throwing superstition around so hard that it almost broke a mirror – before walking onstage to a standing ovation. He performed for twenty minutes, and it was terrific. He improvised almost the entire set. He then told the audience he had to leave to bring on an act. This didn't go down so well. He then brought me on to what can only be described as indifference. The audience wanted to know why someone they knew from off the telly had now been replaced by a complete stranger. My first five minutes was a real struggle – bear in mind I was only doing a maximum of ten. I then started to get bigger laughs, but it was all too late. My time was up. As Michael came back onstage and shook my hand his eyes seemed to say, 'Well, we gave you a shot.'

Suffice to say I wasn't chosen for the programme. The act after me was though. Was it because by then the audience had understood what was happening a bit more, was it because he was half my age or was it simply because he was better then me? I didn't know and still don't, although I know which reason I'd prefer . . .

As if this weren't punishment enough to my ego, I had decided to write a new show for the Edinburgh festival. Some of it would continue where the previous one finished and would therefore include the making of the documentary, the arrest and the 'fraudulent' information on the CRB report. The show would also be about the fact that my book had now been turned down by five major publishers, each one stating that, although it was well written, funny, entertaining, etc., etc., unfortunately I was the wrong gender. I wanted to tackle sexism from a male point of view – even though I was fully aware there would be fewer examples. The show was called *Bennett Arron Has Had Enough!* The tagline was 'Arrested in a dawn raid by CID, told that his novel can't be published because he's not a woman and discovered his friend is on a better mobile-phone tariff . . . Bennett Arron has had enough!'

I was splitting a run at the Edinburgh Festival with Robin Ince. Neither of us wanted to do a full month – I didn't want to be away from the family for so long – so it worked out perfectly.

As with my first show, I had managed to find a sponsor for this one. This time it was the credit reference agency

Call Credit – the company for which Owen, whom I had met on the *Lorraine* programme, worked.

A week before the show I went to Spain with Rosy and the children. I then left them there, with Rosy's parents, while I went to Edinburgh for two and a half weeks. The show went generally well. The second half, the story of the documentary and the arrest, was better received than the first. No one seemed that interested in the fact that I couldn't get my book published or the whole 'inequality' thing in general. I wondered if they didn't feel they 'should' agree with it, or whether it just wasn't interesting or funny enough. However, a routine about the programme *Loose Women* went well, as did an anecdote about the time I worked for one day as a gravedigger!

Although the show was full to capacity every night and I had some great reviews, I decided that this would be my last Edinburgh.

As before, news of this show travelled by word of mouth and I was subsequently asked to perform it in Glasgow, Sheffield and . . . Australia.

I had been asked by the organisers of an information security conference in Australia (AusCERT) if I would be one of their guest speakers. I was delighted. The only slight problem was that the conference was to take place in four weeks' time!

A fee had been agreed and I was asked if I wanted to fly business class, or go economy and keep the difference. I chose the latter. Regardless of how uncomfortable I would be, I could easily spend the twenty-five hour flight, each way, working out how to spend the extra money!

A week before I was due to fly out the organisers

suddenly realised that I needed a work visa which, I was told, would normally take up to two months to arrange. So I didn't think I'd be going after all.

However, the people who were running the conference had 'connections', and within three days I had a visa! What efficiency.

Initially I had been booked as the speaker for the end of the day. This is where I'm usually placed at conferences as my talk generally puts people into a good mood before drinks and socialising. However, they had been let down by their opening speaker and asked me if I would do that slot instead. The opening keynote conference speaker. At 9 a.m. In front of 1,500 delegates. For an hour.

What could I say?

Well, I suppose I could have said no, but that would have seemed rude.

I was flying to Brisbane, only stopping at Singapore airport en route for four hours. I had never travelled this far before. I had been to Los Angeles, Dubai and Las Vegas, but this was substantially further. I tend to suffer from claustrophobia, which isn't an advantage when you're stuck for twenty-five hours in a metal tube. Fortunately I had no one sitting next to me so it wasn't as bad as it could have been. Also, I had the excitement of the trip to keep me going. And I had a plan as to how I was going to spend my time on the plane. I was going to work for the first couple of hours, then allow myself a glass of wine, watch some films and have a sleep. However, from the moment we took off and the flight attendant asked me if I wanted a drink, the whole plan fell apart.

Spending virtually a whole day on an aeroplane is just

weird. There are only so many Adam Sandler films you can watch before wanting to grab a parachute and force open the door. I found myself looking forward to mealtimes – like a schoolchild or a hospital patient. I did manage to work on a script and look over my talk and I did manage to sleep in short bursts. However, every time I woke up I looked at my watch, hoping it would be later than it was.

During the flight I constantly had this odd feeling that people were looking at me. At first I thought it was because I was, again, one of the few who had ordered a vegetarian meal or because I never let the drinks trolley pass without sampling some of its delights. But it also happened on the few occasions when I was neither eating nor drinking.

When we eventually disembarked in Brisbane, this feeling continued. The company had sent a driver for me – well, actually they had sent one for Arron Bennett according to his sign, but I decided to take it anyway. It was a long drive to the hotel, so the driver and I had a lovely chat, during which he asked me why I was there. I told him about the ID theft and the documentary.

'Oh, that's where I recognise you from!'

I was as surprised to hear this as you no doubt are reading it.

Apparently my documentary was one of the pro-gramme options on Australian flights. That's why people had been looking at me. It also explained why I'd occasion-ally received emails from people asking me what happened at the end of the programme as they had left before seeing it. I'd assumed they'd just gone out – although I was never sure why they simply hadn't recorded it.

It was nice to hear that the programme had reached a

wider audience, but disappointing that, although I had directed and presented the programme, my fee (all £1,500 of it!) was a buy-out so I would never receive royalties.

I arrived at the hotel around 8 p.m. – which for me was 10 a.m. after a largely sleepless night. I was met by Claire, the woman who had booked me, and she immediately invited me to join her for a drink in the bar where she could introduce me to everyone. I was exhausted, but I knew that if I went to bed straight away I wouldn't sleep much as my mind would believe I was just having an early nap. So I said that I would shower and change and then join them for an hour or so. I checked into my room. I mean, suite. Yes, they had booked me an incredible suite overlooking a golf course. I wished I was staying for longer than four days. A month would have been ideal.

The 'hour or so' which I had intended to spend at the bar with my hosts turned into several hours. Everyone wanted to buy me a drink and then tell me which was the best Australian beer and why. I chatted and played pool until 1.30. I was the first to leave the party, but then I was the one who would be giving a presentation seven hours later . . .

Although I only managed about three hours' sleep, the adrenalin of standing in front of 1,500 people kept me wide awake. I had never performed comedy that early before (although, on British time, it was more or less when I usually perform) and as I was the first speaker of the day, and some of the audience looked a little hungover, I didn't think it was going to be easy.

The first few jokes, my usual preamble before getting into the story, didn't get much of a response. This didn't bode well. However, once they realised that this wasn't going to be a 'normal' presentation, they tuned in more. It eventually went down very well and I had some great reactions. As usual, at one point I asked if anyone had been arrested. Generally when I ask this, one or two people put up their hand. There, it must have been about fifty!

There were some great questions at the end too, especially from representatives of the Australian police.

After the talk, Claire told me that there had been some press interest in my visit and asked if I was happy to be interviewed. Both myself and my ego were very happy. Identity Theft was a growing crime in Australia, but hadn't yet reached the scale it had in the UK and the US. My story, and documentary, were therefore of interest.

I was interviewed for the evening news and also for one of the biggest Australian newspapers.

That evening I was taken out for drinks by some of the organising team. We went to a few cocktail bars and were about to go into a large sports bar when I was stopped by the bouncer and told to remove my hat. I like wearing my hat. It's my . . . thing. Some people believe I wear it because I'm losing my hair (and perhaps need somewhere to keep it), but that's not the case. Rosy had once seen a hat in a shop and thought it would suit me. So I used to wear it occasionally – but never for gigs. Then one night before a gig I was shaving my hair (a number-two) and, as I was about to put the razor away I noticed that I had missed a bit on the side. So I went to shave it – completely forgetting that I had removed the plastic grading attachment. So I ended up with a wide bald line across the side of my head. I screamed and Rosy and the kids came running upstairs, assuming I had at least cut an ear off. I didn't want to go onstage looking like that, so I wore my hat. The moment I wore it onstage I loved the feeling. It sounds silly, but I had always been looking for a 'thing'. This was it. And I had become accustomed to wearing a hat all the time – excluding in bed and in the shower – so being told to remove it always annoyed me. As is what happened in Australia. I asked why and I was told that was the rule. Always a great explanation. Now, I could have just removed it and gone into the bar. But being told a rule is a rule because it's a rule does tend to irritate me. So I abandoned the sports bar and, with a couple of sympathetic delegates in tow, made my way back to the hotel, where we again played pool into the early hours.

That night I couldn't sleep at all. The jet lag was affecting me badly, and even though I was exhausted, I could not rest for more than half an hour before waking up. Bored and irritable, I switched on the television. As the screen flickered to life and I saw the images come into focus I genuinely thought I was mid-dream. Or at least having a jet-lagged hallucination. There, on the television, in Australia, at 4 o'clock in the morning, was Swansea City football team, the team I support, playing against Nottingham Forest. The time difference had completely thrown me and I thought the match was on the following day. The winner of this match would go to the play-offs at Wembley for a place in the Premier League. My tiredness and lack of sleep were forgotten as I sat, then stood, on my bed watching the match unfold.

My excitement grew as Swansea took the lead. I promised myself that if Swansea were to win, Xander and I would go to Wembley. When the final whistle blew, with the score 3–1 to Swansea, I was literally jumping up and down on my bed – not a pleasant sight, to be honest, as I don't tend to wear pyjamas when I stay in a hotel.

I immediately texted a friend of mine in Swansea and asked him if he could get me two tickets. He said he would look into it.

Unsurprisingly, this added excitement didn't really help with my sleep. So I went downstairs – yes, I dressed first – in the hope someone might still be around for a game of pool. Who was I kidding? Of course people were still around. In fact, the group I'd been with earlier had only just returned from the sports bar so were happy to share in my excitement.

When I woke up the next morning, afternoon, evening . . . whenever it was, I did feel a little worse for wear. But happy. That night I was due to perform at their awards ceremony. It was a large event, with around 2,000 people. The fantastic comedienne Corinne Grant was hosting it, and the winners of *The X Factor Australia* were also on the bill. I only had to perform for ten minutes, and I had been working out which material to do. I obviously wasn't going to repeat anything I had mentioned in the Identity Theft talk the previous day.

Once my head cleared, I sat in the room thinking about which material would work best for that audience. As I was going through my set, I received a message from Paul, the lawyer. We had finally received notification that the CRB information had been altered. I was both pleased and irritated. Pleased that it had at least been corrected, but irritated that it had happened in the first place and that, once again, no one would be blamed for anything and there would be no repercussions for anyone.

While reading this message from Paul, I received a call to

the room. I answered the phone and was greeted with the words 'Hello, Mr Arron, just to let you know your massage is ready in the spa.'

I thought for a moment. I knew I'd had a little too much to drink the previous night, but I had no recollection of booking myself a massage. I'd occasionally, in the past, drunkenly and hungrily ordered late-night room service without consideration for the ridiculous expense and 'tray charge', but ordering a massage? That was a whole different level.

'Er . . . when did I book this?' I asked, trying not to sound like a lunatic.

'You didn't, Mr Arron. It's been booked for you by the organisers of the conference.'

'Oh. Right. Yes. Okay. I'll come down now. Thank you.'

Although I was relieved that I hadn't been massage-bookingly drunk, a new emotion hit me. One of . . . nervousness.

This is probably going to sound odd, but not only had I never had a massage before, I had never wanted one. But I couldn't think why. I knew I was against having one, but was not aware of any rationale behind this. So I thought, it might not only help with the remnants of the hangover and the jet lag, but could also relax me for the performance that evening. So I went.

The spa area was lovely. I was taken into a room, given a towel, told to remove my clothes and then to lie down on my stomach. I did as I was told. As I lay there, listening to whale calls and wondering if whales ever listened to humans calling each other, I tried to remember what my issue had been with massages. The masseuse then arrived and introduced herself. She told me what she would be doing – it was like an anaesthetist prepping you before an operation. When she finished she asked me if I understood. I wondered how often people said, 'Sorry, you lost me after oils and hot towels . . .'

So she started the procedure. And it was incredibly relaxing. As she rubbed my neck she told me that I was very tense. This made me tense. She then commented on this. It was a relaxing vicious circle. As she did her job, we chatted a little. She told me how long she had been a masseuse and what her qualifications were. She then asked me what I did for a living. This is always a question I find weird to answer. I don't know why. It's probably because it's such an odd profession. Many times at social events I've told people I'm an estate agent just to avoid the 'Tell us a joke', 'Here's one for you', 'Who's your favourite comedian?' or, my personal favourite, 'You'll probably use this as part of your routine.' Anyway, I decided this was too intimate a situation to lie so I told her I was a comedian. She told me that she loved British comedy and that she was a big fan of Ricky Gervais. I told her that I had supported him on a couple of warm-up tour shows – well, she had been showing off about her job! She told me that she loved *The Office*, and we chatted about comedy for a while.

After about ten minutes she lay some small hot towels on my back and then told me that she was going to leave me for a few minutes and then come back and remove them. I was feeling so relaxed that I almost didn't have the energy to voice my understanding.

She left the room and I continued to do nothing. Why had I been so worried about this? What was wrong with having a massage? Why did . . . ?

That's when I remembered.

After being kicked out of drama school and before teaching at the girls' school, I had needed a job. At the time, pizza delivery was quite a new concept and they were looking for people who had their own vehicle. I had a car so I applied for a job at a pizza company in Camden, north London, and was successful in my application. I had apparently answered all the questions correctly. These had ranged from 'Do you have a car?' to 'Do you want to deliver pizza?'

It was a fun job and, as it was still quite a novel concept, I'd occasionally be invited in to people's houses for a drink. On one particular evening, I delivered a large vegetarian to a 20th birthday party in Kentish Town. (I obviously mean a large vegetarian pizza, not just a large vegetarian.) The birthday girl asked me in for a drink and introduced me to her friends. I stayed for a while, drinking, dancing and sharing the pizza I had brought. I then suddenly remembered that I had another pizza to deliver, which I had left in the car. I quickly left, checked my *A–Z* and drove to the other customer. I was an hour late as I knocked in the door. It opened and a huge – I mean 'huge' – man stood there. I immediately burst into tears and told him that the reason I was late was that there had been a horrific accident, I had been the only witness and I'd had to wait for the police to arrive and give them a statement. I then described in detail, through my sobs, the extent of the accident and how many had been killed. At the end of the story I handed over the cold pizza and told him that he had every right not to pay me. Not only did he pay me, but he gave me a large tip.

So drama school hadn't been a complete waste of time . . .

You are probably wondering what this has to do with the massage. Well, the last pizza I ever delivered was to a massage parlour on Camden High Street. I arrived at the dark, damp-smelling place with two pizzas and handed them over, together with the bill. An elderly lady who was standing behind a counter took the boxes and looked at the bill.

'Oh, this is more than I expected,' she said. I wasn't sure how to respond. Surely she'd had a menu which clearly stated the prices.

'Perhaps . . .' she continued, 'we could come to an arrangement.'

At first I wasn't sure what she meant. Honestly. I thought she was looking at some kind of hire purchase deal whereby she'd pay in weekly instalments over the next month. She then rang a bell and two young girls, who could easily have caught colds, walked into the room.

'Maybe we can help?' they suggested.

I was about to explain that I didn't really have the time or inclination for a massage, when, eventually, I suddenly realised what was on offer. I thanked them and declined in the same breath. I then told them not to worry about the pizza and quickly left.

I arrived back at the pizza company, about to tell my colleagues my story, only to find my boss and co-workers laughing loudly. My natural paranoia led me to assume they were laughing at me, so I was both pleased and annoyed when I discovered this was the case. They explained to me, between pauses for guffawing, that they had known exactly what was going to happen, as this was an 'arrangement' they had with the girls. A pizza in exchange for . . . well, you can guess.

So, there I was, in this beautiful hotel in Australia, lying face down, virtually naked save for a scattering of small warm towels, wondering if the masseuse was going to offer me anything else. I kept dismissing the thought as ridiculous. After all, this was a classy hotel. That wasn't going to happen here. Surely she'd lose her job. Then I thought about all the businessmen she would be dealing with here. Maybe there was a look or a nod that signalled an 'understanding'. If so maybe I had inadvertently given the signal.

I once again dismissed my stupidity.

Then I thought . . .

But it was too late. The door had reopened and the masseuse, who in half my mind was now a prostitute, walked back in. I turned my head to look at her and she smiled.

No! Was that the sign?!

She closed the door, picked up some massage gel, looked at me and said; 'So . . . what about 'extras'?'

I knew it! I'd been right. Or at least half of me had been. It was the Camden pizza scenario all over again.

I sat up – which resulted in most of the towels falling to the floor – and said, 'Look, you're very attractive, but I only wanted a massage. In fact I didn't really want that, to be honest, but it had been paid for. And this might have been paid for too, which would be weird, but I still don't want anything else, thank you.'

There was an uncomfortable pause as she looked at me. At first there was confusion, then a look of hurt and upset.

'No . . .' she said, 'I . . . I just wondered what you thought of it. I really enjoyed it, but . . . I still prefer *The Office*.'

Chapter 18

Despite the massage incident, the time in Australia really was great. My stand-up bit at the awards show went really well and I was given various business cards for other potential events. On my way back I was again recognised by several people in the airport and on the aeroplane, but this time it was because there was a full-page article about me, complete with photo, in the newspaper.

When I returned home I was feeling quite positive. This positivity increased when a producer, who potentially wanted me to be a presenter on a new consumer show, approached me. She had two other presenters in place; one was an ex-con-artist who had turned good guy and the other was a female presenter who was currently working on a daytime TV show. The working title of the show was *Scam School* (marginally better than their original idea of *My Big Fat Scam*.)

Over the next few weeks I went in for several, unpaid, meetings, gave loads of ideas and filmed some 'scams'. I then waited to hear. After several weeks and telephone calls I was told, by one of the researchers – the producer wouldn't speak to me herself – that they were very grateful for my input and suggestions but they had decided not to use me. I sent them an invoice for my work.

Neither the payment nor the programme ever appeared.

Speaking of reformed ex-con-artists, the large security company McAfee had asked me to appear at an event. I was to be one of several speakers, and I would be going on before Nick Leeson – the person who famously brought down Barings Bank.

I had been adding material to my talk and I was now able to perform for anything from twenty minutes to an hour and a quarter. They just wanted thirty minutes. I have to say, this thirty minutes went down very well, mainly as I criticised the police and the postal system and there were representatives of both in the room! I then stayed to watch Nick Leeson, who gave a great talk.

Afterwards, at the 'drinks and mingle', Nick came over to me and told me how much he had enjoyed my talk. I didn't even know he'd watched it. He asked me if I was interested in working together. Me and Nick Leeson – together at last! I told him that I would love to and he said he'd introduce me to his agent. A couple of days later he invited Rosy and me to watch him at 'An Evening with Nick Leeson' in a hotel in Mayfair. We dressed smartly, obviously, and attended the event.

There was a lovely champagne and canapés reception beforehand, of which Rosy and I took full advantage. The evening was in two halves and, just before the interval, Nick told the audience that there would be a surprise guest speaker in the second half.

In the interval I asked Nick who the guest speaker was going to be.

'You,' he replied, looking confused. 'I told you.'

I explained that he hadn't mentioned it at all. He

apologised and said he thought he had. He asked me if it would be okay. I wasn't sure. His agent then came over and explained how this would be a perfect opportunity for them to see me perform. I felt I had little choice. So, after the interval – which lasted substantially longer than twenty minutes, due to the sheer number of people enjoying the free bar – Nick went back on and introduced me to the audience.

As is the norm at these types of events, I started off with some 'normal' stand-up – which went down okay – and then went into the Identity Theft material. Unlike my stand-up, this is a story with funny material, but it's not all gag, gag, gag. It has moments of pathos and on more than one occasion I have actually seen people cry (which I hope is because of the emotional content and not because they want it to finish). It does therefore require a little bit of concentration. Unfortunately the audience that evening, which consisted predominantly of drunken bankers and their drunken partners, wasn't in the mood to concentrate. And told me so. Loudly. So, in between telling the story as best I could to those who were interested, I found myself dealing with a constant barrage of heckles. Fortunately, having been a stand-up comedian for so long and having played many of the toughest clubs in the country, I was able to retaliate. The problem now was that this was the bit they were enjoying. So little by little my routine and story fell by the wayside as I battled with the audience. Still, Nick and his agent were impressed, and I did subsequently have work from some members of the audience who contacted me later.

I'd enjoyed performing at Nick's evening and it made

me start thinking about performing another solo show –
even though I'd said I'd never do one again.

But what would I talk about? I had already done one and
a half shows about Identity Theft so I didn't feel I could touch
on that subject again – even though it was so important to
me. However, even though I couldn't speak about Identity
Theft, I did want to talk about my identity. As I said earlier,
I always talk about my identity onstage and mention that I
am both Jewish and Welsh. So I wanted the show to be all
about this. I decided on the title *JEWELSH*.

Robin Ince asked me if I would again like to share a run
of our shows at the Edinburgh Festival. I agreed – once I'd
chatted about with Rosy who was amazed, and slightly
disappointed, that I was considering doing this again.

As with my previous show, I went on holiday with Rosy
and the children to Spain beforehand and left them with
Rosy's parents while I ventured to the colder climes of
Scotland.

In the show I talked about my family roots, mainly because
years ago my father told me a story that I wanted to tell
onstage. My father had grown up in a very observant house-
hold. Religious Jews are not allowed to do any type of work
on the Sabbath. Lighting a fire constituted work. So each
religious family would therefore have someone, a non-Jew,
to light their fire for them. The person who used to light my
grandparents' fire every Saturday was a young boy who was
the son of the local baker. This young boy was, incredibly,
Anthony Hopkins. Yes, Hannibal Lecter lit my grandparents'
fire. (I actually considered this as the title of the show!)

I genuinely didn't know if anyone would be interested in
this show. It was quite a personal thing and I suddenly

wondered whether anyone who wasn't either Jewish or Welsh or both – which would be limiting - would turn up.

However, I was pleasantly surprised. Again each show was full to capacity and I had some of the best reviews I've ever received. One publication gave me four stars and the reviewer stated that he would have given me five, had I not kept my hat on indoors while there were ladies present. I felt I was being reviewed by a publication from the 1800s.

As a result of my Identity Theft show, I had been asked to make a documentary. As a result of this new show I was again approached by a production company with a view to making a documentary. Unlike the first time, however, this time I was much more sceptical.

They had seen *How to Steal an Identity*, and wanted to know if I was interested in making a programme in which I traced my family's roots from Lithuania to South Wales and looked into the reasons for the decline of the Jewish population in Wales. Like most people, I had always been interested in finding out more about my background and where I came from. Ever since I'd had my identity stolen, this was something I wanted to do more. I know there's no logical reason for this, but psychologically it had become even more important.

I had long telephone conversations with the producers, who were probably wondering why I wasn't jumping for joy. The thing was, after my last experience of making a documentary, I had to be sure nothing detrimental would happen and that I wouldn't be 'made' to do anything. Assurances were given and we worked on an outline for the programme. Although I wouldn't be directing this time, there was still a lot of work for me to do.

I knew there had at one time been a large Jewish

community in the South Wales valleys and I was interested to know what had happened to them. So there was a lot of research and preparation to be done.

While I was working on the programme, a representative from the Royal Mail Group contacted me and booked me into visiting several of their offices to perform my Identity Theft show. They particularly wanted me to speak with the Postal Redirection Department to show them what can happen if they don't carry out their task correctly. (Remember, I'd arranged to have my post redirected from a previous address, but they had allowed something to slip through, which had started all the problems.) They also asked me make an in-house video for them.

Although the research and preparation for this new documentary took a while, the filming was all done in a week – slightly less than the year and a half it had taken to make *How to Steal an Identity*. It was also really enjoyable, even though some of the things I discovered were upsetting. Many Jews had escaped the pogroms – the anti-Jewish riots – in Russia and surrounding areas in the late early 1900s and came to South Wales, either because they had family there or, if the mythology is to be believed, because they thought they had arrived in New York.

Years after they had arrived and settled, anti-Semitic riots once again forced them to leave their homes . Fearing for their safety, some Jews then hid their identities. Having your identity taken from you is one thing, having to hide it for fear of your life is . . . I honestly can't think of a suitable adjective.

Part of this documentary showed me performing my *JEWELSH* show. I had wanted to show some stand-up in my first documentary but hadn't been allowed, so I was delighted it was in this one. I was also delighted that the majority of the audience for the filmed show was made up of old school friends, the majority of whom I hadn't seen since I was eighteen!

After the show we all chatted and reminisced. It really was a great evening, even though to be honest I didn't remember everyone! My dad was there too, which made the evening even better – especially as it had been a good show.

I was very pleased with the finished programme. The only thing with which upset me slightly was that they decided to only show it in Wales as, according to the commissioner, 'No one would be interested outside Wales.' I don't think this is true at all. But, as usual with these things, my view is irrelevant. The programme was called *The Kosher Comedian*. I didn't mind the title but I'd preferred the one I'd suggested, which was 'Jew Do You Think You Are?'

So, several years after having my identity stolen and then making a documentary on the subject, I had now made another programme which dealt with the importance of identity. However, this time I wasn't arrested for my efforts.

Epilogue

At the end of my Identity Theft shows I have a Q&A session. I'm usually asked, amongst others, three questions.

These are:

1. What can be done to stop Identity Theft?
2. Did they ever catch the person who stole my identity?
3. Am I pleased with what I did?

My answers are:

1. Nothing. We can cut the chances of it happening, but we can't completely stop it. It's one of the fastest growing crimes and it looks as though it's going to continue that way. As I've shown, we, as individuals, are sometimes careless with our information and either give it away or throw it away too easily. However, companies are at fault too. They send out junk mail and take on new customers without proper, rigorous checks. We are sometimes told by financial institutions that, if money is fraudulently taken from our accounts, we won't be liable for it

and it will be replaced. But by then it's too late. Once your credit rating has been affected, you will have real problems.

2. No, they didn't. I know his name, but for legal reasons I'm not allowed to say it. All I can say is that his name is an anagram of 'steals people's identities'. If you add some letters and take some others away.

3. Although I would have preferred for my identity not to have been stolen in the first place, yes, I am pleased with what I have done. I'm pleased that I have made more people aware of the severity of the crime, and I'm pleased that, because of what I did, they had to make an alteration to the process of applying for a UK driving licence. It now clearly states on page three of the driving licence application form: 'As birth certificates are not absolute proof of identity, you must also send one other form of identification.'

So I am pleased with what I have achieved and I'd like to think that I have made some sort of difference. Who knows, maybe that difference will stop you from having your identity stolen.

Thank you for reading my book. Whoever you are.